THE OFFICE GUIDE TO
MODERN ENGLISH USAGE
SECOND EDITION

JEAN C. VERMES
CAROL M. BARNUM, PH.D.

MJF BOOKS

NEW YORK

Published by MJF Books
Fine Communications
Two Lincoln Square
60 West 66th Street
New York, NY 10023

ISBN 1-56731-224-1

The Office Guide to Modern English Usage
Copyright © 1981 by Parker Publishing Company, Inc.
Copyright © 1991 by Prentice Hall, Inc.

This edition published by arrangement with
Prentice Hall/Career & Personal Development

This book was formerly published as *The Secretary's Guide to Modern English Usage*

Manufactured in the United States of America on acid-free paper

MJF Books and the MJF colophon are trademarks of Fine Creative Media, Inc.

10   9   8   7   6   5   4   3   2   1

Introduction to Second Edition

What you say and how you say it, whether your communication be written or spoken, reflects not only on yourself but on the company you represent. That's why it is so important for you to be aware of and practice good speaking and writing skills for effective business communication.

The second edition of this popular and practical handbook for secretaries keeps the spirit of the first but is revised to bring you the latest developments in business practice and technology. The impact of the electronic office on your job is addressed throughout this book to give you current information on new formats, new methods of communicating in business, and new vocabulary.

The original format of the first edition is retained. The book is divided into three sections: Part I on effective speech, Part II on effective writing, and Part III on effective letters. However, the focus has been expanded and new features added to answer the sometimes confusing questions and changes affecting contemporary business practice.

- When, for instance, is it appropriate to use *Ms.*? What if a woman prefers *Mrs.* or *Miss*?
- Is it appropriate to address a group as Gentlemen or Sirs?
- Which letter formats are the most popular today?
- What specialized vocabulary should a secretary be familiar with?

- How has the impact of computers affected the secretary's job?

In addition to these new features, the second edition contains updated information on many of the most popular features of the first edition. These include information on

- How to pronounce common business terms.
- How to divide compound words.
- How to address military and government personnel.
- How to abbreviate words in business usage.
- How to avoid jargon and clichés that may be outdated or inappropriate.

You'll even get the answers to tricky questions of word choice, such as when to use *good* or *well* and when to use *bad* or *badly*.

The answers to these and many other questions are contained in the pages of this revised second edition. Your access to them is easy with the Find-o-matic look-up system developed for the first edition. Using this system, you can quickly scan the table of contents for the specific information you need, and then scan the left margin of the text for the corresponding number of the section you want.

You'll also want to use the handy charts reviewing the highlights of each section. You may want to copy and post these near your desk for instant reference or expand them to include other points you want to remember. Sample charts include Pronunciation Reminder, Spelling Tips, and Three Handy Rules of Grammar.

In your role as a secretary, you are a vital link in the communication system. You're often the first contact people have with your company, and you may be the chief communicator for your boss. The better you are at what you do, the better your company will feel about you and the better you will feel about your professionalism and skills. *The Secretary's Modern Guide to English Usage*, second edition, can be an indispensable part of your career success, as it is designed to make your job easier and more rewarding.

Carol M. Barnum, Ph.D.

Contents

Part II
EFFECTIVE WRITING   75

PART I

EFFECTIVE SPEECH

1

Pronunciation and Enunciation

First impressions are vitally important, especially for a secretary. In your various business relationships you project an image, not only of yourself, but also of your immediate superior and of your firm as a whole. Associates judge you by your grooming, your clothes, and your speech. No matter how perfect your appearance, you can spoil the entire effect with slurred enunciation and mispronounced words. Everyone gets careless in this respect occasionally, sometimes without being conscious of it.

1:1   BE CAREFUL, YOUR DICTION IS SHOWING!

Make it a point to listen to your own speech for just one day. You may be surprised at some of the speech habits you may have adopted. Watch out particularly for the following:

Expression	Translation
Cancha	Can't you
Woncha	Won't you
Idonwanna	I don't want to
I'm gonna	I am going to
I'll meecha	I will meet you
Lessgo	Let's go
Watchawant	What do you want

Other speech habits that you may find yourself unconsciously using are the dropped g's in words such as "doin'," "seein'," and "goin'," as well as "len'th" and "stren'th." Do not, however, try to counteract your slurred speech with exaggerated emphasis. Reclaim the lost consonants but do not stress them as in "doingh," "seeingh," or "goingh."

Above all, do not sound the *t* in the group of words ending in **sten** or **ften**. The *t*'s should never be sounded in the following:

Fas(t)en
Lis(t)en
Has(t)en
Of(t)en
Sof(t)en

After enunciation comes a more complicated problem—pronunciation. In a country as large as the United States, there are some regional differences in pronunciation. The dictionary itself gives second choices in pronunciation for a number of words. The first choice should be used unless you are someplace where certain words are pronounced differently and another pronunciation would make you sound snobbish or affected.

1:2 THE RADIO ANNOUNCER'S TEST

A number of words that are commonly mispronounced have been gathered into a paragraph that is used on radio as an announcer's test. Try it and see how well you can score on the boldface words before looking at the answers that follow.

The old man with the **flaccid** face and **dour** expression **grimaced** when asked if he were **conversant** with **zoology, mineralogy,** or the **culinary** arts. Not to be **secretive**," he said, "I may tell you that I'd given **precedence** to the study of **genealogy.** But since my father's **demise,** it has been my **vagary** to remain **incognito** because of an **inexplicable, lamentable,** and **irreparable** family **schism.** It resulted from a **heinous** crime, committed at our **domicile** by an **impious** scoundrel. To **err** is human . . . but this affair was so **grievous** that only my **inherent acumen** and **consummate** tact saved me."

Correct Pronunciations

flaccid	FLAK-sid, FLAS-id
dour	DEW-er, DOW-er
grimaced	grim-AYCED, GRIM-ist
conversant	CON-versant, con-VER-sant
zoology	ZOE-ology
mineralogy	miner-AL-ogy
culinary	CUE-linary, KUL-inary
secretive	se-CREE-tive, SEE-critive
precedence	pre-SEED-ence, PRES-edence
genealogy	jeeny-AL-ogy, jenny-AL-ogy
demise	de-MIZE
vagary	va-GAY-ry, VAY-gary
incognito	in-COG-nee-to, incog-NEE-to
inexplicable	in-Explicable, inex-PLICK-able
lamentable	LAM-entable, la-MEN-table
irreparable	ir-REP-arable
schism	SIZZ-em, SKIZ-em
heinous	HAY-nus
domicile	DOM-isile, DO-misile
impious	IM-pius, im-PIE-us
err	EHR, UHR
grievous	GREE-vus
inherent	in-HEHR-ent, in-HEER-ent
acumen	a-CUE-men
consummate (adjective)	CON-sum-mit, con-SUM-it

Counting one point for each word pronounced correctly, a score of 21 to 25 indicates that you need to consult a dictionary or pronunciation list only occasionally. A score of 15 to 20 is good, but you must watch yourself carefully, check when in doubt, and learn a few rules that will help you determine how certain words should be pronounced. As you can see from the alternate pronunciations for so many of these words, it helps to check the dictionary often.

1:3 FOUR EASY PRONUNCIATION RULES

Unfortunately, all pronunciation rules have exceptions, but here is a good general guide.

1:3a Words Ending in ABLE

Words of more than two syllables ending in *able* are usually accented on the first syllable. Even with this rule, however, some words now have two acceptable pronunciations. **Hos-PIT-able and La-MENT-able are two examples.**

AM-icable	FOR-midable
AP-plicable	HOS-pitable
COM-parable	LAM-entable
DES-picable	PREF-erable
EX-plicable	REP-utable
REV-ocable	

Exceptions: When a prefix is added to any of the foregoing words, the accent remains on the originally stressed syllable, which now becomes the second syllable: in-AP-plicable, in-COM-parable, in-EX-plicable, in-HOS-pitable, dis-REP-utable, ir-REV-ocable, ir-REP-arable.

1:3b Words Ending in ATE

In words ending in *ate*, the last syllable in the noun or adjective sounds like *it*, while the last syllable of the verb sounds like *ate*.

	Noun or Adjective	Verb
advocate	advo-kit	advo-cate
alternate	alter-nit	alter-nate
articulate	articu-lit	articu-late
associate	associ-it	associ-ate
consummate	consum-mit	consum-mate
degenerate	degener-it	degener-ate
delegate	dele-git	dele-gate
deliberate	deliber-it	deliber-ate
elaborate	elabor-it	elabor-ate
estimate	esti-mit	esti-mate
graduate	gradu-it	gradu-ate
importunate	importu-nit	importu-nate
intimate	inti-mit	inti-mate
moderate	moder-it	moder-ate
precipitate	precipi-tit	precipi-tate
separate	sepa-rit	sepa-rate
subordinate	subordi-nit	subordi-nate
syndicate	syndi-kit	syndi-cate

Exceptions

Nouns

candi-date
concen-trate
de-bate
re-bate
poten-tate

1:3c Words Ending in ILE

In words of more than one syllable ending in *ile,* the last syllable is usually pronounced *ill.* (If you have heard English actors pronounce it to rhyme with *smile,* that is because British pronunciation differs from the American in certain respects.) However, many of these words are acceptable with either pronunciation. Again, when in doubt, check your dictionary.

agile	mercantile
docile	puerile
fertile	servile
fragile	sterile
futile	textile
hostile	versatile
juvenile	virile
*mobile	volatile

*Mobile, in some uses, is pronounced "mo-beel."

These exceptions end as in *smile.*

compile	infantile
crocodile	profile
defile	senile
*domicile	turnstile
exile	

*Domicile is sometimes spelled **domicil** and pronounced like **ill.**

1:3d Words Pronounced According to Use

A two-syllable word, used as both noun and verb generally is accented on the first syllable for the noun and on the second syllable for the verb.

Noun	Verb
CON-duct	con-DUCT
IN-sult	in-SULT
PER-fume	per-FUME
PROG-ress	pro-GRESS
REF-use	re-FUSE

Exceptions: Preface, comment, and **trespass** are accented on the first syllable, whether used as nouns or verbs. **Crusade, decline,** and **dispatch** are all accented on the last syllable, whether used as nouns or verbs.

1:4   101 FREQUENTLY MISPRONOUNCED WORDS

A desk dictionary is an essential part of any secretary's equipment for checking spelling and pronunciation when in doubt. In many cases, however, you may be mispronouncing without being aware of your mistakes. The following list gives the preferred pronunciation according to several popular dictionaries. Alternate pronunciations are sometimes acceptable, but the preferred one should be your choice, except in those cases where a very common alternative pronunciation is given.

A

abdomen	AB-do-men
affluent	AFF-loo-ent
appellate	ap-PELL-it
athlete	ATH-leet

B

bade	BAD
beautiful	BYOO-tih-full
bicycle	BY-sickle

C

chauffeur	show-FUR
chiropodist	kih-ROPP-o-dist
clandestine	clana-DESS-tin

D

dais	DAY-is
data, datum	DAY-ta, DAT-a (plural), DAY-tum, DAT-um (singular)
divers	DY-verz (several)
diverse	dih-VERS, DY-vers

E

emeritus	eh-MERR-ih-tus
erudite	ERR-yoo-dite
exigency	EK-sih-jen-sy
exquisite	EKS-kwi-sit

F

facetious	fah-SEE-shus
February	FEB-roo-erry
finance	fih-NANS
fracas	FRAY-cus

G

gamut	GAMM-ut
garage	gah-RAZH
gibberish	JIB-er-ish

H

harass	HAR-ass, ha-RASS
hedonism	HEE-don-izm
heinous	HAY-nus
humble	HUMM-b'l

I

incognito	in-KOG-nih-to
indigent	IN-dih-jent

J

jocose	joe-COSE

K

kiln	KILL, KILN
kilogram	KILL-o-gram
kilometer	KILL-o-meter
kimono	kih-MOE-nuh

L

largess	larr-ZHES
larynx	LARR-ingks, LAR-ingks
leisure	LEE-zher
liaison	LEE-a-zon, lee-A-zon
lichen	LYE-ken

M

marquis	MAHR-kwis, mark-KEE
methane	METH-ane
morale	mo-RAL
morass	mo-RASS
mores	MOE-reez
mundane	mun-DANE

N

nadir	NAY-der
naive	nah-EVE
naphtha	NAFF-tha
nomenclature	NO-men-klay-ture

O

obligatory	ah-BLIG-ah-tory
ornate	or-NATE
overt	oh-VERT

P

paradigm	PAR-a-dime
perjure	PURR-jer
prelate	PRELL-it
prelude	PRELL-yood
prerogative	preh-ROGG-ah-tiv
pristine	PRISS-teen
propane	PRO-pane
pumpkin	PUMP-kin

Q

querulous	KWER-uh-luss
quietus	kwy-EE-tuss
quinine	KWY-nine

R

rapport	rah-PORE
rarity	RARR-i-tee
recluse	reh-KLOOS, REK-loos
redress	reh-DRESS
relapse	reh-LAPS
requisite	REK-wih-zit
respite	RESS-pit
romance	ro-MANS

S

sadism	SAD-iz'm, SAY-dizm
salient	SAY-li-ent
satyr	SAY-ter
schism	SIZ-em
sinecure	SIGH-neh-cure
sojourn	SO-jurn
subtle	SUT'l

T

teetotaler	tee-TOE-t'ler
termagant	TUR-mah-gant
theater	THEE-ahter
thesaurus	theh-SAW-rus
trachea	TRAY-key-a
turbine	TUR-binn

U

ubiquitous	yew-BIK-wih-tus
ultimatum	ul-tih-MAY-tum
umbrella	um-BRELL-ah
untoward	un-TOW-erd
usury	YEW-zhe-ree

V

vagary	vah-GAR-ee, VAY-gah-ree
valet	VAL-ett, va-LAY
verbatim	vur-BAY-tim
verbiage	VER-be-idj
virago	vih-RAH-go

W

wisteria	wi-STEER-ee-ah
worsted	WOOS-ted, WUR-stid
wreak	REEK

Z

zoology	zoe-OLL-o-ji
zucchini	zoo-KEY-nee

1:5   SEVEN SECRETS OF CORRECT PRONUNCIATION

Here are seven simple ways to correct common flaws in pronunciation. Once you become aware of them, you will find your diction immeasurably improved.

1:5a   Sounds That Are Often Omitted

First and most important, you must watch out for slipshod pronunciation that leaves out vowels and consonants intended to be heard, as in **arctic,** which should be pronounced "AHRK-tic," not "AHR-tic." A few samples will illustrate.

	Right	Wrong
artists	AHR-tists	AHRtis
asked	ASKT	AST
candidate	KAN-dih-date	KAN-ih-date
fifth	FIFTH	fith
government	GUV-ern-ment	GUV-er-ment
height	HITE	hithe

	Right	Wrong
hundred	HUND-red	HUN-red
language	LANG-gwij	LANG-wij
length	LENGKTH	LENTH
liable	LYE-a-b'l	LYEb'l
library	LYE-bray-ry	LYE-berry
quantity	QUAN-tih-ty	QUAN-it-ty
recognize	RECK-og-nize	RECK-uh-nize
surprise	sur-PRIZE	supp-RIZE
temperature	TEMP-er-uh-cher	TEMP-uh-cher

1:5b Sounds That Are Unnecessary

Another careless speech habit is the addition of sounds that do not belong. Saying "ATH-a-lete" instead of "ATH-lete" is a common example of this mistake. Some others are as follows:

	Right	Wrong
disastrous	dih-ZAS-trus	dis-ZASTER-us
entrance	ENT-rance	ENTER-ance
equipment	ee-QUIP-ment	ee-QUIPT-ment
grievous	GREE-vus	GREE-vee-us
hindrance	HIND-rance	HIND-er-ance
laundry	LAWN-dry	LAWN-der-ry
mischievous	MIS-chih-vus	MIS-chee-vi-us
modern	MOD-ern	MOD-er-an
monstrous	MONS-trus	MONS-ter-us
remembrance	re-MEM-brance	re-MEMBER-ance
umbrella	um-BRELL-la	um-BEREL-la

1:5c Substitute Sounds

Many words are mispronounced because the speaker substitutes the wrong sound for the correct one. For example, someone might say "ab-SORB-shun" instead of "ab-SORP-shun" for the word **ab-sorption**, which is spelled with a *p*, not a *b*. The following are frequently mispronounced in this way.

	Right	Wrong
architect	AHR-kih-tekt	AHR-chi-tekt
category	CAT-eh-gory	CAT-ah-gory
chiropodist	kih-RAHP-uh-dist	chi-RAHP-uh-dist
congratulate	con-GRAT-u-late	con-GRAD-u-late
frustrated	FRUS-tray-ted	FLUS-tray-ted
Massachusetts	MASS-ah-CHEW-setts	MASS-ah-TOO-setts
nuclear	NEW-clee-ur	NEW-cue-ler
percolate	PER-kuh-layt	PER-kyoo-layt
radiator	RAY-di-ay-ter	RAD-i-ay-ter
ribald	RIB-l'd	RYE-bawld
similar	SIM-ih-lar	SIM-ul-ar
strategy	STRAT-eh-ji	STRAD-eh-ji
statutes	STACH-oots	STACH-oos

1:5d Transposed Sounds

Inversion is the reversing of the sequence of two letters in a word. One such inversion always got a laugh on television. When Archie Bunker said "PRE-vert" instead of "PER-vert" for the word *pervert,* it made the rest of us feel superior, because we knew better. We may unconsciously be making similar mistakes ourselves without realizing it. Here are a few.

	Right	Wrong
ask	ASK	aks
bronchial	BRONK-ee-al	BRONIK-al
larynx	LARR-inx	LAR-nix
modern	MOD-ern	MOD-ren
prefer	pre-FER	per-FER
perform	per-FORM	pre-FORM
perspiration	pers-pir-A-shun	pres-pir-A-shun

1:5e The Silent Letters

Letters which are not pronounced are called *aphthongs.* Most of us don't say "AN-ti-kyoo" for *antique,* except in jest. We know it is pronounced "an-TEEK," but some of the other examples may be less obvious.

	Right	Wrong
apropos	ap-ruh-POE	ap-ruh-POZE
asthma	AZ-muh	AZTH-muh
boatswain	BO-sun	BOAT-swain
butte	BYOOT	BUHT-ee
camomile	CAM-o-mill	CAM-o-mile
comptroller	kun-TRO-lur	comp-TRO-lur
corps	KAWR	KAWRPS
debris	dah-BREE	dah-BRISS
Des Moines	Dah-MOIN	Dah-MOINS
forte	FORT	for-TAY (except in reference to music)
gnome	NOHM	guh-NOH-mee
Illinois	Ill-in-NOY	Ill-i-NOISE
indict	in-DITE	in-DIKT
jamb	JAM	jamb
palm	PAHM	PAHL'm
phlegm	FLEM	FLEG'm
proboscis	pro-BAHS-is	pro-BAHS-kiss
starboard	STAR-bird	STAR-board
viscount	VYE-count	VISS-count

1:5f   Misplaced Accents

Accenting the wrong syllable is one of the most common pronunciation mistakes. As you know, words ending in **able** are usually accented on the first syllable. There is no other rule to follow in pronouncing words of more than one syllable. It is a matter of remembering the correct accent through frequent use.

The following words are accented on the first syllable.

	Right	Wrong
alias	AY-lee-us	uh-LYE-us
backgammon	BAK-gam'm	bak-GAM'n
Broadway	BRAWD-way	brawd-WAY
impotent	IM-po-tent	im-PO-tent
ignominy	IG-nuh-min-y	ig-nuh-MIN-y
orator	AWR-a-tor	aw-RAY-tor
vehement	VEE-he-ment	ve-HEE-ment

The following words are accented on the second syllable.

	Right	Wrong
cigar	sih-GAR	SEE-gar
clandestine	clan-DES-tin	CLAN-des-tine
condolence	kon-DOHL-ens	KAHN-duh-lens
defeat	dih-FEET	DEE-feet
distributive	dis-TRIB-u-tiv	dis-tri-BEW-tiv
exemplary	ex-EM-plary	EX-em-plary
municipal	myoo-NIS-i-p'l	myoo-ni-SIP'l
police	po-LEES	PO-lees
remonstrate	reh-MAHN-strayt	REM'n-strayt
superfluous	soo-PER-floo-us	soop-er-FLOO-us

1:5g The Secret of Simplicity

In their efforts to pronounce words correctly, some people go overboard and acquire affected pronunciations that they imagine are upper class. In the following list, a number of the affected pronunciations would be correct British English, but if you're not British, using them sounds peculiar.

	Normal	Affected
after	AFF-ter	AHF-ter
editor	ED-ih-tur	ED-ih-tawr
either	EE-ther	EYE-ther
fortune	FAWR-chin	FAWR-tyoon
illustrate	ILL-us-trate	ih-LUS-trate
isolate	EYE-so-late	ISS-uh-late
lute	LOOT	LYOOT
menu	MEN-yoo	MAY-noo
negotiate	ne-GO-shee-ate	ne-GO-see-ate
profile	PRO-file	PRO-feel
process	PROSS-es	PRO-ses
sacrifice	SAK-ra-fice	SAK-ra-fiss
secretary	SEK-ra-terry	SEK-ra-tree
simultaneous	sy-mul-TAY-neus	sim-mul-TAY-neus
stew	STOO	STYOO
vitamin	VY-ta-min	VIT-a-min

Some words have different pronunciations for different regions of the country. In these cases, follow the practice of your region.

Pronunciation Choices for Different Regions

aunt	ANT	AHNT
either	EE-ther	EYE-ther
neither	NEE-ther	NYE-ther
pecan	PE-can	pe-CAHN
potato	po-TATE-o	po-TAH-toe
tomato	toe-MAY-toe	toe-MAH-toe
*vase	VAZE	vahz

*Some people claim that an inexpensive vessel is pronounced VAZE and an expensive one is pronounced VAHZ. Again, let regional reference be your pronunciation guide.

1:6 WORDS WITH A FOREIGN ACCENT

Many words used in English speech are of foreign origin, usually Greek, Latin, or French. When *ch* has a hard sound, the word is of Greek or Latin derivation. When *age* has a soft sound, the word comes from the French.

1:6a Words Containing CH

	Right	Wrong
Achilles	a-KILL-eez	a-CHILL-eez
archives	AHR-kives	AHR-chives
chameleon	ka-MEE-lee-on	cha-MEE-lee-on
chaos	KAY-os	CHAY-os
chasm	KAS'm	CHAS'm
Chianti	kee-AHN-tee	chee-AHN-tee
zucchini	zoo-KEE-nee	zoo-CHEE-nee

1:6b Words Containing AGE, EGE, or IGE

Words of French derivation ending in *age, ege,* or *ige* have a soft sound.

	Right	Wrong
barrage	ba-RAHZH	ba-RAHDJ
cortege	cor-TEHZH	cor-TEHDJ
menage	meh-NAHZH	meh-NAHDJ
sabotage	SAB-a-tahzh	SAB-a-tahdj

The pronunciation of some words is changing to allow for a hard or soft sound at the end, as in the following examples:

camouflage	KAM-eh-flahzh, KAM-eh-flahdj
corsage	cor-SAHZH, cor-SADJ
garage	ga-RAHZH, ga-RAHDJ
massage	ma-SAHZH, ma-SAHDJ
prestige	pres-TEEZH, pres-TEEDJ

2

Vocabulary Enlargement

The English language contains hundreds of thousands of words, not to mention the number of specialized and technical words increasing daily. You cannot expect to learn all of these, and there is no reason why you should. Twenty to thirty thousand words are adequate for the average high school or college graduate. These comprise the words you use yourself or recognize when others use them.

2:1 HOW TO RATE YOUR VOCABULARY

You cannot compute the exact size of your own vocabulary, but you can get a general picture of its extent by rating yourself on the following tests. Counting one point for each word you know, 18 is an average score, 25 is a very good score, and 35 is a superior score. (The answers are at the end of this chapter.)

2:1a Multiple Choice

Describe the function of each person listed:

1. An apothecary

   a. utters wise sayings
   b. mixes drugs
   c. abandons his or her faith

2. A chauvinist
   a. drives a car
   b. hates women
   c. believes in the superiority of his or her own group

3. A cosmopolite
   a. travels the world
   b. lives in the city
   c. is very sophisticated

4. An entomologist
   a. studies words
   b. studies insects
   c. studies human beings

5. A flautist
   a. flouts society
   b. plays the flute
   c. shows off

6. A gaucho
   a. is an acrobatic dancer
   b. herds cattle
   c. is tactless

7. An optician
   a. is an eye doctor
   b. measures visual defects
   c. grinds lenses

8. An orthopedist
   a. specializes in children's diseases
   b. treats foot troubles
   c. treats bone disorders

9. A philatelist
   a. engages in love affairs
   b. donates to charity
   c. collects stamps

10. A raconteur
    a. tells stories well
    b. sings on the stage
    c. is engaged in illegal business

2:1b   Opposites Attract

Decide which of the following words are similar in meaning and which are opposite:

1. acute	sharp	obtuse
2. brave	cowardly	courageous
3. candor	frankness	hypocrisy
4. effect	cause	consequence
5. fictitious	true	false

6. incarcerate   imprison   liberate
7. judicious   irresponsible   sagacious
8. lustrous   glossy   opaque
9. nefarious   virtuous   wicked
10. taciturn   garrulous   reticent
11. timorous   intrepid   craven
12. verbose   wordy   speechless

2:1c The Match Game

Match the words in column A with the correct meanings in column B.

A	B
1. ascetic	a. about to occur
2. cajole	b. hidden
3. ecstatic	c. coax
4. feign	d. stiff
5. fluster	e. pretend
6. gaudy	f. disloyalty
7. imminent	g. restore to useful life
8. latent	h. confuse
9. perfidy	i. flashy
10. prosthesis	j. cleanse
11. purge	k. severely austere
12. rehabilitate	l. extremely enthusiastic
13. rigid	m. artificial replacement device
14. synthetic	n. substitute for the real thing

2:2 ADD A WORD A WEEK

Learning new words indiscriminately accomplishes little. The words you learn should add variety to your usual conversation and be suited to your needs. When reading, watching television, or conversing, if you come across a word you believe you could use appropriately, make a note of that word.

2:2a Look It Up

As soon as you have the opportunity, look up the word in the dictionary for exact spelling, meaning, and pronunciation. Do not attempt to use the word until you are absolutely sure of what it means and how it should be pronounced.

For example, you could very well refer to a **Freudian slip** as "FROO-de-an" instead of "FROY-de-an," or describe a singer as a "PRY-ma-donna" instead of a "PREE-ma-donna." If you decided to use the word raze after hearing someone say, "They razed the building," you might assume that *raze* meant to put up when it actually means to tear down.

2:2b Write It Down

We have all looked up the same word over and over again each time we see it or hear it because we cannot remember its meaning. We have not written it down to imprint it on our memory. Write down any word you want to remember on a three by five card or notepad with correct spelling and pronunciation indicated and a brief summary of its meaning. Keep this collection of words in a desk drawer where you can refer to it frequently and memorize the words before attempting to use them. For example:

Spelling:	en•er•vate
Pronunciation:	ENN-er-vayte
Meaning:	exhaust or weaken

2:2c Put It to Work

Some words would not fit in with your daily conversation, but you want to understand them. These words, like **androgyny, eponymous,** or **paradigm,** are part of what is known as your recognition vocabulary, which won't be put to frequent use. Any word that is to become a part of your spoken vocabulary must be used often in order to remain there. If you want to learn a word a week, you must put those words to work. One of the easiest ways to pick up new words that fit into your usual conversation is to vary your usual speech with synonyms for words you already use.

2:3 80 PAIRS OF SYNONYMS AND HOW TO USE THEM

Synonyms do not necessarily have exactly the same meaning. It is these variations that make your speech more interesting. For instance, when you ask, "Do you want to *add* to that statement?" it means, "Have you any additions?" If you ask, "Do you want to *amplify* that statement?" it means, "Do you want to give it a fuller treatment?"

Here are some synonyms, listed in pairs, with definitions.

relevant has a bearing on the matter
pertinent has a logical and precise bearing on the matter

pretend to assume something falsely (implies no evil intent)
feign to assume falsely some condition to evade responsibility

prevent to take direct counteraction to stop something from happening
preclude to make impossible by previous action

unique the only one of its kind (cannot be qualified by degree)
unusual uncommon in amount or degree

presume to guess at something being possible without full knowledge (may imply an unwarranted conclusion)
assume to take something for granted without proof (but sometimes on safe grounds)

use to employ or apply for a particular purpose (also to take advantage of)
utilize to use to produce results

anxious worried or apprehensive about some uncertain event
eager impatiently expectant of some anticipated event

clandestine secretive action to conceal something illegal or improper
covert any act not taken openly

flaunt to exhibit ostentatiously
flaut to defy openly

indifferent not partial or biased
uncaring having a lack of concern

satisfactory acceptable to those for whom it is done
adequate equal to some requirement

adjacent near one another
adjoining meeting at a boundary line

beautiful that which stirs a heightened response of the senses
and the mind
lovely that which appeals to the emotions rather than the
mind

behavior action in the presence of others
deportment behavior as related to a set of rules

bright shining with original or reflected light
brilliant unusually bright

cancel to cross out with lines, to invalidate
eradicate to remove all traces

continual repeated regularly and frequently
continuous repeated in unbroken succession

danger exposure to possible evil
peril exposure to imminent evil

arduous demanding a great effort and endurance
difficult hard to achieve

ambiguous having two or more possible meanings
equivocal capable of different interpretations

example represents something of which it is a part
sample an actual part of something larger

administer to carry out
execute to have charge of or to manage

fear emotion aroused by the presence of danger
apprehension uneasiness or dread about the future

vascillate to swing indecisively from one course of action or
  thought to another
fluctuate to rise and fall like waves

general belonging to all of a class or body
universal found everywhere and with no exceptions

anguish an agonizing physical or mental pain
grief deep mental anguish from loss or misfortune

happy enjoying a pleasure or joy
jovial having a joyous humor

malevolence having the desire to harm others
hatred intense aversion

idle not in use, unemployed
indolent lazy

important significant
momentous of extreme importance

congenital existing at birth
inherent naturally existing in something

knowledge understanding gained through experience or study
erudition profound knowledge, often in a specialized area

large of more than ordinary size
gigantic exceedingly large

quiescent motionless, in a state of inaction
latent hidden from ordinary observation

credible worthy of belief
likely very probable

make to cause to exist or to happen
fabricate to construct something by combining or assembling

melody simple harmonic composition
tune the entire melody

motley a variety of parts, emphasizing the differences (often expresses contempt)
miscellaneous made up of a variety of parts, similar in kind but defying classification

avaricious greedy for money
miserly tending to hoard money

blend to make a harmonious mixture
mix to put together indiscriminately

morose sudenly melancholy
acrimonious bitter

mysterious something secret, arousing wonder or curiosity
inscrutable difficult to understand, puzzling

native belonging by birth or origin (native country)
indigenous native to a country or location (like a plant)

essential   that which cannot be removed or left out for something to exist

necessary   that which fills an urgent need

neglect   failure to take reasonable care

negligence   regular habit of neglecting something

abstruse   difficult to understand

obscure   difficult to see

obsolete   gone out of use

obsolescent   going out of use

perverse   wrongly self-willed or stubborn

obstinate   refusing to change

elderly   past late middle age

old   having lived or existed for a very long time

comprehend   to grasp mentally

perceive   to become aware of directly through the senses

fracas   a disorderly fight

quarrel   an angry dispute in word or action

persist   adhere to a course or opinion (usually negative)

persevere   persist in the face of obstacles (usually positive)

question   an interrogation calling for a reply

inquiry   a close examination that seeks information or truth

pity   feeling of grief for the misfortunes of others

compassion   pity plus a desire to help

cite   to mention or refer to some source when the reference is not exact

quote   to present another's exact words

rare seldom found
unique one of a kind

similarity a surface likeness in several characteristics
resemblance a likeness in appearance only

recover to obtain again after a loss
retrieve to recover by effort

infallible absolutely trustworthy, incapable of error
reliable having qualities on which you can depend

sad sorrowful or unhappy
dejected a temporary state of discouragement

reticent disposed to be silent, reserved
taciturn habitually untalkative, uncommunicative

combine to put together
unite to form a larger or stronger unit

transient remaining only a short time
transitory short-lived or impermanent

oral pertaining to spoken words only
verbal pertaining to words, written or spoken

cautious guarding against possibilities of danger
vigilant on the lookout against danger

youthful possessing or suggesting youth or vitality
juvenile mentally or physically immature

violent involving great force or feeling
furious very violent

work exertion of body or mind
labor hard manual work

learning acquired knowledge
wisdom good judgment, common sense

wit quick perception and amusing response
humor like wit, but more kindly in response

ability the power to do something
capacity the condition that permits one to acquire the power

normal conforming to a typical pattern or type
average typical, commonplace

usual customary, ordinary
habitual settled or constant from habit

can implies ability
may requests permission

common belonging to two or more
mutual reciprocal, something given and received

compare to note likeness or difference
contrast to distinguish differences

persuade to influence to action
convince to overcome doubts

imply to suggest without actually stating
infer to draw a conclusion based on evidence

confirm to remove all doubt about a matter previously in
   doubt
validate to establish a conclusion by evidence or
   demonstration

2:4 TIPS ON SAYING WHAT YOU MEAN

We are all guilty of using ambiguous language, especially spoken language, which we have no chance to study and correct. We often say "biannual" (twice a year) when we mean "biennial" (once in two years), or we say "bimonthly" (once in two months) instead of "semimonthly" (twice a month).

2:4a How to Avoid Ambiguous References

Pronouns like *this, which, they, that,* or *it* are often used in a way that causes confusion. Consider the following example:

- We get a lot of rain in the summer, which kept children indoors. *This* caused a problem for many parents.

What does *this* refer to? It's not quite clear since it generally refers to everything in the previous sentence. It's better to clear up the problem by attaching the pronoun to a specific noun:

- We get a lot of rain in the summer, which kept children indoors. *This rainy weather* caused a problem for many parents.

Here's a sentence with a slightly different problem, using the pronoun *it:*

- In this morning's paper, *it* talks about the accident on Elm Street.

It has no specific reference. For clarity, rewrite the sentence:

- This morning's paper had an article about the accident on Elm Street.

Other examples of the problem with ambiguous pronouns are as follows:

Confusing:	Ms. Dennis is going to Canada. They are interested in hiring her.
Clear:	Ms. Dennis is going to Canada. A Canadian firm is interested in hiring her.
Confusing:	I can't give you that information until Mr. Evans gets back, which is unfortunate.
Clear:	Unfortunately, I can't give you that information until Mr. Evans gets back.
Confusing:	Mr. Fawcett promoted Mr. Graves after he had worked here for only six months.
Clear:	Mr. Fawcett promoted Mr. Graves after Mr. Graves had worked here for only six months.

Another common ambiguity is the misuse of pronouns, as in the following sentence:

- May talked to Ruth about the way *she* planned to improve the filing system.

The listener does not know who is going to improve the filing system, May or Ruth. In such cases, you must repeat the name of the person to whom you refer.

- May talked to Ruth about the way May planned to improve the filing system.

2:4b Correct Word Usage

Still another ambiguity arises from carelessness in word usage, as illustrated in the following instances:

alternative An *alternative* is one of two possibilities. If there are more than two, it is preferable to refer to three, four, or more *choices.*

among *Among* refers to more than two persons or things, as in "*among* the three of us," not "*between* the three of us." See *between*.

amount *Amount* refers to a certain quantity, while *number* refers to things that can be counted: "There was a large *amount* of money," or "There were a large *number* of bills."

balance   When speaking of money, you say, "The **balance** is due." Otherwise say, "the **remainder** of the shipment," rather than "the **balance** of the shipment."

between   **Between** refers to two people: "**between** you and me." See **among.**

biweekly   This means every two weeks. Use **semi-weekly** for twice a week.

bring   **Bring** indicates movement toward the speaker: "**Bring** the invoice to me." Otherwise, use **take:** "**Take** this report to the supervisor." See **take.**

consensus   Since **consensus** means a generally shared opinion, it is redundant to say "consensus of opinion."

criterion   **Criterion** is a test by which something is measured. **Criteria** is the plural and should not be used in place of the singular.

datum   **Data** is the plural form and **datum** is the singular. "Here are the **data.**" The word is in transition, however, and "Here is the **data**" is gaining acceptance. For the present, however, it is best to use the proper form.

everybody   **Everybody** is singular and takes a singular pronoun: "**Everybody** brought **his or her** (not their) notes to the meeting." Other singular pronouns include **anyone, everyone, and someone.**

former   **Former** refers to the first of two things. **Latter** refers to the second of two things. When discussing more than two things, use **first** and **last.**

graduate   A person **graduates from** a school or is **graduated from** a school. "She **graduated** high school" is not considered correct.

hanged   A person is **hanged.** A mirror is **hung.**

individual   This means a particular human being, distinguished from a group. **Person** is preferable when the meaning is general.

join together   Since **join** means "to put or bring together," it's redundant to add "**together.**" Just use **join,** except in a marriage ceremony.

kind *Kind* is singular, and *kinds* is plural. Refer to *that kind* or *those kinds,* never *those kind.* The same is true for *sort* and *sorts.*

latter The second of two things. See *former.*

lend *Lend* is a verb: "Please *lend* (not loan) me your pen." See *loan.*

less *Less* means "not so much" and refers to single items, like *less* milk, *less* money. Use *fewer* when referring to plural items, like *fewer* glasses of milk, *fewer* dollars.

loan *Loan* is a noun: "I am applying for a *loan."* See *lend.*

media This is the plural of *medium.* Newspapers, radio, and television are the *media.* However, like *date, media* is gaining acceptance as a singular word.

none Traditionally, this is a singular work requiring a singular verb: *"None is* going." However, it is now generally considered correct to use *none* as a plural when it is followed by a plural noun or pronoun: *"None* of the members *have* their badges."

number *A number* is generally plural: *"A number* of items **are** missing." *The number* is generally singular: *"The number* of items *is* large."

party This should refer to more than one person, except in telephone or legal usage.

phenomena This is the plural of *phenomenon.* Do not use it in a singular sense. Say, "one such *phenomenon,"* or "several *phenomena."*

regard *Regards* means good wishes and should not be used in place of *regard,* which means reference: "In *regard* to the matter we discussed."

rob A person is *robbed* usually by force or through an act of violence. A possession is *stolen.*

take *Take* indicates a movement away from where you are. See *bring.*

temperature Degree of warmth or coldness. You *take* your temperature. You don't *have* a temperature. If your temperature is high, you have a *fever.*

2:5 CHECKING YOUR BUSINESS VOCABULARY

Certain words that are rarely used in ordinary conversation are commonplace in business. Some apply only to special kinds of business, like *codicil* (law), *prognosis* (medicine), or *galley* (publishing). Others are common to most businesses, like *follow-up*, *tickler*, *collating*, *data processing*, and *word processing*.

2:5a General Business Vocabulary

Here are a few words relating to the conduct of business:

accrual   increase by natural growth

adjournment   postponement of a meeting

affidavit   statement that is written, signed, and sworn to

agenda   digest of matters to be treated at a meeting

amortization   gradual, periodic payment of a debt

bylaws   rules adopted by a corporation to regulate its conduct

capitalization   total amount of a corporation's securities

collateral   something of value deposited as a pledge

collating   checking sets of typed pages for numerical sequence

combing back   moving forward reminders of matters requiring attention

conference call   a multiparty telephone call that connects people at different locations so they can hear and speak to each other at the same time

consignment   shipment of goods by owner to selling agent

consolidation   combination of two or more corporations

controller   chief accounting officer
(comptroller)

data processing   process by which data are received, stored, rearranged, and transmitted

debentures   bonds issued without security

depreciation   loss of value

electronic mail transmits messages composed on the computer of the sender to the computer of the receiver, who checks his or her "mailbox" to read the mail (commonly called E-mail)

equity net worth

escrow conditional delivery of something to a third person

facsimile a copy of a document transmitted electronically over telephone lines from one facsimile machine to another, where it is then printed out (commonly called a fax)

fiscal period period covered during one cycle of business operations

follow-up system method of filing material so it will be brought to someone's attention at a certain date

hardware the computer and associated equipment directly involved in the performance of communications and data processing

incorporated organized into a corporate body

indemnification reimbursement for litigation expenses

indexing arranging files in alphabetical or numerical order

injunction a writ by a court of equity, commanding someone to do something or restraining them from doing something

insolvent without the funds to pay debts

interface relationship; also used informally as a verb to mean "interact"

inventory all the goods awaiting sale

liabilities debts or obligations of a business

lien a charge making property a security for an obligation

liquidation distribution of assets of dissolved corporation to stockholders

markdown a reduction below original retail price

markup difference between cost price and selling price

minutes official record of proceedings at a meeting

modem a device that converts computer transmission to telephone transmission so data can be sent along telephone lines to another computer

motion formal proposal for the consideration of those present at a meeting

negotiable capable of being legally transferred from one person to another

notarize to acknowledge or attest a document, as done by a notary public

novation substitution of a new contract for an existing one

offset printing through a photographic process

option an agreement to hold an offer open for a certain period

peripheral an auxiliary device, such as a printer, that works in conjunction with a computer

personnel the body of persons employed by a business

photocopy duplication by copy machine

photostat reproduction by the same principle as photography

portfolio list of securities owned by an individual or a company

posting transferring debit and credit entries to proper accounts in a ledger

proxy person with authority to vote for an absent stockholder

quorum number of persons who must be legally present at a meeting

ratio the relation of one quantity or value to another

routing preparing the mail to go to the persons by whom it should be read

screening procedure to protect executives from handling unimportant phone calls

software a computer program that performs a specific task

spread sheet an array of values organized in rows and columns, allowing for the analysis of information, commonly available in computer software

subpoena an order commanding a person to appear in a legal proceeding

teleconference telephone and/or video connections between two or more locations to allow for a long-distance meeting or presentation

telemarketing the use of the telephone to make marketing and sales calls to large numbers of potential customers

tickler a reminder system

voice mail allows users to record a message in their own voice and to receive messages from others using a push-button telephone (functions like an answering machine)

wire transfer a common banking practice that allows for the rapid electronic transfer of money from one account to another, especially useful for out-of-state transactions

word processing computerized system that allows documents to be printed, stored, and retrieved later for revision

yield annual percentage of return on an investment

2:6   232 SPECIALIZED BUSINESS WORDS AND EXPRESSIONS

In addition to the general business vocabulary listed in the previous section, every business and profession has specialized words that are peculiar to itself. Typical examples include *arraignment* in law, *fluoroscope* in medicine, and *galley* in publishing. Here are eight groups of such words that you may encounter at some time in your working life. If you do not know the meaning of the specialized words in your field of work, you'll want to look them up in a dictionary and make them part of your vocabulary.

2:6a   Accounting

accrual	depreciation	ledger
auditor	disbursements	liabilities
capitalization	fiscal	revenue
depletion		

2:6b   Computing and Management Information Systems

Ada	directory	mouse
backup	field	operating system
BASIC	file	parallel port
bit	floppy disk	Pascal
boot	FORTRAN	pipe
byte	mainframe	RAM
C	memory	ROM
Central Processing Unit	microcomputer	serial port
chip	modem	sort
COBOL	monitor	surge protector
data base		

2:6c   Investment and Finance

amortization	collateral	negotiable
annuity	convertible	portfolio
bearish	debentures	pyramiding
bill of sale	escrow	underwriter
blue-sky laws	junk bond	yield
bullish		

2:6d   Insurance

actuary	cancellation	liability
adjuster	coinsurance	mortality
assessment	disability	rider
assignment	endowment	salvage
beneficiary	floater	subrogation

2:6e   Law

abatement	eminent domain	notarize
actionable	garnishment	statutory law
admissible	guaranty	subpoena
antitrust	indemnification	suretyship
arraignment	injunction	testimonium clause
attestation	interstate commerce	tort
bailment	intrastate commerce	usury
bankruptcy	legal tender	waiver
codicil	negotiable instrument	warranty
decedent	nonnegotiable instrument	writ

2:6f Medicine

abscess	diabetes	pituitary
acupuncture	diathermy	placebo
adrenal	electrocardiogram	prognosis
alimentary	electroencephalogram	prophylaxis
antibiotic	embolism	psoriasis
bacteriology	emollient	psychiatrist
barbiturate	fibrillation	psychosomatic
cardiograph	fluoroscope	purgative
cathartic	hemoglobin	surgeon
catheter	hemmorrhage	therapy
cerebral	neurology	

2:6g Publishing

agate	dummy	lowercase
appendix	font	offset
artwork	format	overlay
bibliography	galley	pitch
boldface	halftone	point
byline	leading	repagination
callout	legend	typography
camera ready	letterpress	uppercase
caption	lightface	videodisc
copyfitting	line cut	viewdata
copyright	linetype	widow
cropping	logo	WYSIWYG (Wizziwig)
desktop publishing		

2:6h Real Estate

amortization	grantee	quitclaim deed
appurtenances	grantor	right of way
attestation	leasehold	sale and leaseback
chattel mortgage	lessee	testimonium clause
conveyance	lessor	vendee
easement	lien	vendor
equity	marketable title	warranty deed
floor/area ratio	mortgagee	zoning
foreclosure	mortgagor	

2:6i Television and Radio

actualities	intercutting	reception
anchor person	master shot	satellite
bird feed	mini-camera	short-form series
bite	newscaster	sitcom
closed caption	newscenter	sound bite
close-up	one-shot	telecast
commentator	pilot	Telstar
coverage	prime time (noun)	transmission
cue card	prime-time (adj.).	voice over
dee-jay	pubcaster	voice wrap
documentary	rebroadcast	whiparound
hot switch		

2:7 WORD ROOTS AS A GUIDE TO WORD MEANING

Prefixes are standard syllables attached to the front of a word to modify its meaning. For instance, the word *restart* is a combination of the root word *start,* meaning "to begin," and the prefix *re,* meaning "again." Thus, *restart* means to "begin again." *Suffixes* are standard syllables attached to the end of a word to modify its meaning and usually its function. For instance, *refrigerate* is a verb meaning "to cool." By adding the prefix *ion,* the word becomes *refrigeration,* a noun meaning "the process of cooling." By changing the suffix to *or,* forming the word *refrigerator,* the meaning changes to "the mechanism that produces cooling." Learning the standard prefixes and suffixes can help improve your vocabulary and spelling.

2:7a Prefixes Showing Quantity

Prefix	Meaning	Example
semi	half	semiannual
uni	one	unicycle
mono, mon	one	monorail, monarch
bi	two	bimonthly
tri	three	tripod
quadr	four	quadrangle
penta	five	pentagon
sex, hexa	six	sextuplets, hexagon

Prefix	Meaning	Example
sept	seven	septuagenarian
oct, octo	eight	octagon, octopus
nona	nine	nonagenarian
dec	ten	decade
cent	hundred	century
milli	thousand	milliliter

2:7b Prefixes Showing Negation

Prefix	Meaning	Example
a, an	without, not	amoral, anorexic
il, im, in, ir, un	not	illegal, immoral, inept, irregular, unknown
non	not	nonconsecutive
ant, anti, contra	opposing, against	antacid, antinuclear, contradict
de, dis	do the opposite	devalue, disapprove
mis	bad	misdemeanor

2:7c Prefixes Showing Time

Prefix	Meaning	Example
ante, fore, pre, pro	before	antecedent, foreground, prenatal, prologue
post	after	postmortem
re	again	reclaim

2.7d Prefixes Showing Direction or Location

Prefix	Meaning	Example
super	above, over	supervisor
sub	below	subordinate
pre	in front of	prefix
ex, e	out	exit, eject
in	into	injection
circum, peri	around	circumference, perimeter
co, con	with	coauthor, consequence

2:7e Common Noun Suffixes

mis**ery**
base**ment**
rele**vance**
operat**or**
play**er**
sister**hood**
particip**ation**
presid**ency**

2:7f Common Verb Suffixes

soft**en**
material**ize**
simpl**ify**
orchestr**ate**

2:7g Common Adjective Suffixes

harm**less**
sel**fish**
petul**ent**
bounti**ful**
ration**al**
circumstan**tial**

2:7h The LY Adverb Suffix

common**ly**
usual**ly**
readi**ly**

ANSWERS TO TESTS

Multiple Choice

1. b		**6.** b
2. c		**7.** c
3. a		**8.** c
4. b		**9.** c
5. b		**10.** a

Opposites Attract

	similar	opposite
1. acute	sharp	obtuse
2. brave	courageous	cowardly
3. candor	frankness	hypocrisy
4. effect	consequence	cause
5. fictitious	false	true
6. incarcerate	imprison	liberate
7. judicious	sagacious	irresponsible
8. lustrous	glossy	opaque
9. nefarious	wicked	virtuous
10. taciturn	reticent	garrulous
11. timorous	craven	intrepid
12. verbose	wordy	speechless

The Match Game

1. k	**8.** b
2. c	**9.** f
3. l	**10.** m
4. e	**11.** j
5. h	**12.** g
6. i	**13.** d
7. a	**14.** n

3

Words and Expressions to Avoid

3:1 CLICHÉS

Clichés, those all-too-familiar words and expressions that we use automatically as part of our vocabulary, can weaken our ability to communicate clearly. When they're fresh and new, clichés make us stop and think about what they mean, but after a while they lose their meaning because of overuse and become merely filler. Take note of the clichés you use during the course of one day, and you will be surprised at their number. You do not need to eliminate them entirely from your speech. Just watch out for the ones you use too frequently. Everyone has his or her favorites. Sometimes there is no other way to say exactly what you mean in the most concise way. For instance, "This car is a *lemon*." Used occasionally and appropriately, clichés can emphasize a point, but you should try to use them with discretion.

3:1a 50 Clichés to Screen Out

acid test	cold as ice
almighty dollar	cool as a cucumber
avoid like the plague	dead in the water
better late than never	dirty old man
bitter end	easy mark
bundle of nerves	flat as a pancake
clear as a bell	fly off the handle

get behind the eight ball

get the ax

go the distance

go to pieces

has a screw loose

head over heels

hit the ceiling

in the same boat

irons in the fire

join the club

know the ropes

let your hair down

live it up

look like a million bucks

make ends meet

method in my madness

misery loves company

never a dull moment

no place like home

no strings attached

old as the hills

on cloud nine

over a barrel

pale as a ghost

perish the thought

put the bite on

red as a beet

ring a bell

ripe old age

sell like hot cakes

shake a leg

shoot the breeze

thin as a rail

turn up your nose

under the wire

with bated breath

3:2 56 Examples of Business Jargon

Businesspeople have their own clichés, like **update** or **finalize.** Like other clichés, these have their uses until they become dated and trite. Try to think of some alternative expressions if you find yourself using any of the following too frequently:

advance planning

all things being equal

at this point in time

auspicious occasion

back to square one

back to the drawing board

ball park

blue sky

bottom line

carry a lot of weight

carry the ball

cash in on

cash on the barrel

ear to the ground

fast-tracker

field of endeavor

finalize

foreseeable future

frame of reference

hands-on manager

hidden agenda

high concept

in the final analysis

kick an idea around

know the ropes

level playing field

moot point

networking

no strings attached	stonewall
nose to the grindstone	streamlining
off the record	swing a deal
ongoing	synergy
operative	take the fall
-oriented (part of compound word)	think tank
pass the buck	touch base
play it by ear	update
power player	upscale marketing
prioritize	upside potential
set up shop	viable option
smart money	whip into shape
soft landing	whole ball of wax
spread yourself thin	window of opportunity

3:3 TIRESOME EXPRESSIONS

In any time period there are words and expressions that turn up in everyone's vocabulary. At first, using them seems fashionable, but after a time they become habitual and tiresome. Here are five that come to mind:

> hopefully
> I couldn't care less
> have a nice day
> meaningful relationship
> beautiful person

These have been used so much that people say them mechanically, with little regard for their meaning. All such words and expressions eventually go out of vogue, and if you get into the habit of using them you are not only lacking in originality, but you are dating yourself as well.

3:3a Hopefully

Hopefully originally meant "with hope" or "in a hopeful manner." Its current usage, to mean "it is to be hoped" or "let us hope," is now generally accepted. Even so, it is overused. For the sake of variety, say instead, "I hope" or "we hope" that a certain event will transpire, rather than "Hopefully, the new campaign will be a success," or "Hopefully, I'll get a raise this year."

3:3b I Couldn't Care Less

I *couldn't care less*, meaning "I really don't care," is not a bad expression; it is just overused. Try to use it less frequently and, above all, don't corrupt it into "I *could* care less." People who use the latter corruption often don't realize that they are actually saying, "I do care somewhat."

3:3c Have a Nice Day

Have a nice day is a pleasant enough greeting, but when everybody says it on all occasions, it becomes a bit ridiculous. Some people vary it with "Have a nice morning" (or afternoon, evening, weekend), which helps, but not much. When one is constantly being told to have a nice day, the phrase can go beyond triteness and become irritating. It is better to omit this or find a substitute.

3:3d Meaningful

A person no longer has a serious love affair; he or she has a "meaningful relationship." People also have "meaningful experiences" or "meaningful dialogues." *Meaningful* conveys a positive feeling toward an experience, a dialogue, or a relationship, but it is rather vague. Be more specific. Have a "serious relationship," an "interesting experience," or a "productive dialogue."

3:3e Beautiful Person

This is another dated generalization. Say instead, "I like her," "I know you'll like her," or "She's very likable."

3:4 SLANG AND ITS USE

Can you remember when everyone was either *uptight* or *feeling groovy,* and people had *hangups* or *good vibes* and *bad vibes*? Such slang expressions should be eliminated if you don't want to seem out of date. Some of them, like *uptight* and *hangups*, are still in use, but it would be evidence of a better vocabulary to substitute more traditional expressions like, "I'm feeling tense," "I'm apprehensive," or "She is so conventional." Instead of referring to *hangups*, describe them as *inhibitions* or *fixations*.

3:4a Dated Slang

Some slang words are shorter forms of expression that have been incorporated into the language, such as **auto, bus, intercom, cab, taxi, exam, phone, piano,** and **zoo.** No one speaks of an **automobile, omnibus,** or **zoological garden** any more. Other slang expressions like **and how!** and **corny** are still used by some people in spite of their datedness, along with **cool, square, far-out,** and **chintzy.** Avoid frequent use of such expressions when they are new, and be the first to drop them when they have been around awhile. They will soon be as antiquated as **cake-eater, cat's whiskers,** and **twenty-three skidoo.**

3:4b Using (and Avoiding) Slang

Slang has its place in spoken English. It can be colorful and fun and show that you're "with it" (to use a slang expression). Members of a group will often adopt a slang language to allow them to talk to each other without those outside the group understanding them. You may want to use some slang expressions just to show that you are a part of this group. But remember that in most professional situations, it is better to use proper English and to avoid slang, except in informal conversations among friends. Some common slang expressions that are widely used are as follows:

get off my back
in the bag
get to first base
beat your brains out
big mouth
a blast
drop dead
to die for
chill out
kick the bucket
rip-off
call it quits
hassle
freaked, freaked out
get off
a drag
hype
get it together
gross, gross out

3:5 BAD HABITS OF SPEECH AND HOW TO OVERCOME THEM

Two extremes of speech are equally bad habits. One is the use of fancy words under the mistaken impression that fancy is better. The other is the use of incorrect words because the correct ones sound strange and you are not in the habit of using them.

3:5a Simple Language Is Best

Many people are under the impression that they need to use fancy words to show how intelligent they are. Resorting to big words when little words would do just as well, or better, often clouds communication, making it difficult for your reader or listener to know what you mean. If you remember that the object of communication is to make yourself clear, then you'll see why big, inflated vocabulary words may do more harm than good. Simple language is best because it is most easily understood by all.

Inflated	Simple
accomplish	do
ameliorate	improve
approximately	about
commence	begin
delineate	outline
effectuate	do
encapsulate	sum up
endeavor	try
enumerate	specify, list
execute	sign
facilitate	help
fastidious	exacting
invidious	offensive
nebulous	vague
penurious	stingy
prior to	before
prioritize	rank
remittance	check, payment
reside	live
secure employment	find a job
subsequent to	after
terminate	end
utilize	use

3:5b Modernize Outmoded Business Expressions

Some business expressions, while still commonplace in letters and memos, no longer reflect contemporary thinking or writing. We often use them without realizing how silly or outmoded they sound.

Outmoded	Updated
We take the liberty	We are
Attached hereto	Attached is
Enclosed herewith, herein	Enclosed is
Enclosed please find	Enclosed is
Hoping for the favor of a reply	I look forward to hearing from you
We wish to acknowledge receipt	We have received
Kindly advise	Please let us know
Your letter of recent date	Your recent letter
We have not been favored with a reply	We haven't heard
We beg to inform you	You will be interested to learn
It has come to my attention	I know (have learned)

The following words should also be avoided. Some are too vague; others are too old fashioned.

> would advise
> contents noted
> under separate cover
> wish to state
> thanking you in advance
> pursuant to
> yours of the 12th
> we remain
> in due course
> as per

3:5c Don't Be Afraid to Speak Correctly

In their zeal to avoid affectation, some speakers deliberately use incorrect words and constructions because they feel that the correct ones sound pretentious. To mispronounce or misuse words deliberately makes you appear ignorant to those who know the correct pronunciation or usage. You'll probably want to add more words to the following list over time.

Incorrect	Correct
ahold of	hold of
ain't	isn't
anyways	anyway
anywheres	anywhere
as to whether	whether
being as, that	since
busted	burst
can't hardly	can hardly
complected	complexioned
could of	could have
drug	dragged
enthused	was enthusiastic
figure	believe, think
fixing to	planning to
gal	woman
guy	man
had ought	ought
heartrendering	heartrending
heighth	height
hisself	himself
I been	I have been
I begun	I began
I done	I did
invite (noun)	invitation
irregardless	regardless
I seen	I saw
kind of	rather
leave	let
liable to	likely to
mad at	angry with
might could	might, might be able
might of	might have
mighty	very, extremely
most	almost
nowheres	nowhere
off of	off
over with	over
providing	provided

Incorrect	Correct
quote (noun)	quotation
reckon	guess
reoccur	recur
she says	she said
snuck	sneaked
start off	start
supposing	suppose
swang	swung
that there	that
theirselves	themselves
them (adjective)	those
this here	this
try and	try to
umble	humble
unawares	unaware
useto	used to
used to could	used to be able
wait on	wait for
youse	you

3:6 FOREIGN WORDS

Many of the words we encounter in business and in conversation are actually foreign words. New words come into the language from many cultures around the world. The ones we're most familiar with are now in American dictionaries. If the foreign word is not well known, it is usually underlined (or italicized) when written or typed.

3:6a Well-Known Foreign Words

The following words have come into English from other languages. You may want to look up the ones you do not know and add them to your list of vocabulary words.

adiós	aperitif	ballet	beau
aficionado	argot	bandeau	belle
à la carte	au gratin	bas-relief	bonbon
à la mode	au revoir	baton	boudoir

bouillabaisse	cognac	loco	résumé
bouillon	coiffeur	lorgnette	revue
bouquet	connoisseur	madame	roué
bourgeoise	consommé	mademoiselle	roulette
bric-a-brac	corps	mañana	sachet
cabaret	crepe	masseur	salsa
café	cretonne	masseuse	seance
Camembert	croquette	monsieur	siesta
camisole	elite	pâté de foie gras	sombrero
canapé	en route	pompon	soufflé
carafe	entree	poncho	suede
chalet	faux pas	portiere	tableau
chamois	fiancé, fiancée	pronto	table d'hôte
chapeau	gourmet	protégé	tango
chateau	hors d'oeuvre	purée	tête-à-tête
chauffeur	jabot	rendezvous	trousseau
chic	julienne	repertoire	

3:6b Specialized Foreign Words

Some specialized words used in business and other applications
come from foreign languages and cultures. These are probably less
well known and should be used with restraint.

Foreign Word	English Equivalent
a priori	existing before some other observation
atelier	workshop or studio
attaché	diplomatic official
au courant	up to date
banquette	upholstered bench
bête noire	someone you fear
bon mot	witticism
carte blanche	unconditional power
caveat emptor	let the buyer beware
ciao	hello, see you later
cominiqué	official report
contretemps	embarrassing situation
coterie	exclusive group

If you choose to use any of these words, you should consult your dictionary for the correct pronunciation.

coup d'état	overthrow of a government by force
coup de grâce	death blow, any finishing blow
de rigueur	strictly required by etiquette
debacle	sudden collapse
dossier	documents on a subject
double-entendre	having two meanings
droit majeure	a primary legal right or claim
élan	spirit, dash
entourage	attendants
entre nous	secretly, between us
fait accompli	accomplished fact
gauche	tactless
gourmand	a person fond of good eating
habeas corpus	a legal document requiring a person to be brought before a judge or court
hauteur	haughty manner
inter alia	among other things
junta	a small group ruling a country after a coup d'état
laissez faire	noninterference in the affairs of others
lingua franca	the language widely used in a particular group
macho, machismo	maleness, virility
maître d'	head waiter or manager of hotel or restaurant
manqué	unfulfilled, fallen short
mea culpa	my fault
memento mori	reminder of death
née	born
nom de plume	pen name
nota bene	note well, take notice
objet d'art	an object of artistic value or curiosity
panache	style
par excellence	superior
pas de deux	ballet dance for two
pièce de résistance	most important item
pied-à-terre	part-time residence

précis	summary
prima facie	at first appearance, immediately clear
Q.E.D.	a Latin abbreviation meaning "that which was to be shown" or "to be demonstrated"
raison d'être	reason for being
savoir-faire	know-how
sine qua non	an indispensable condition
Sturm und Drang	storm and stress, turmoil
tabula rasa	a clean slate, a mind not affected by experiences
trompe l'oeil	visual deception, fooling the eye

4

Sentence Structure

Spoken English is more informal than its written counterpart, but it should still be grammatically correct. You can end a sentence with a preposition without sounding illiterate, and it is perfectly all right to use contractions like *don't* and *won't*.

If a secretary were to say, "Mr. Axelrod *will not* be in this afternoon, and I *do not* expect him until Wednesday," it might give the impression of extreme formality almost to the point of coldness.

Likewise, "This is the person *to whom* I was speaking" might sound affected compared with the informal, "This is the person I was speaking to."

4:1   10 WAYS TO SAY THINGS BETTER

Your speech should be conversational but correct. Double negatives should be avoided, along with other improper usages. The following sections describe simple remedies for correcting 10 typical mistakes.

4:1a   Avoid Double Negatives

Two negative words in the same statement produce what is known as a double negative. This usage was acceptable in Shakespeare's time, but it is considered poor English today.

Incorrect:	I can't find that memo **nowhere**.
Correct:	I can't find that memo **anywhere**.
Incorrect:	I **can't hardly** read his writing.
Correct:	I **can hardly** read his writing.

4:1b   Use Correct Past Tense

There are several mistakes you could make with the past tenses of verbs. First, you might use the past participle instead of the past tense. Take the verb *to see* as an example:

Present Tense:	I **see** the new supervisor over there.
Past Tense:	I **saw** the new supervisor yesterday.
Past Participle:	I **have seen** the new supervisor every day.

The confusion of *saw* with *seen* is a common mistake.

Incorrect:	I **seen** the new supervisor yesterday.
Correct:	I **saw** the new supervisor yesterday.

Another such error adds *ed* to verbs that should form their past tense by a complete change in spelling.

Incorrect:	My friend **drawed** me a map.
Correct:	My friend **drew** me a map.

4:1c   Modify Verbs with Adverbs

We often confuse adjectives and adverbs in our daily speech. An adjective should modify only a noun or pronoun. Do not use an adjective to modify a verb.

Incorrect:	He **dictates** too **rapid**.
Correct:	He **dictates** too **rapidly**.

4:1d   Modify Adjectives with Adverbs

Do not use an adjective to modify another adjective.

Incorrect: This is a **real good** typewriter.
Correct: This is a **really good** typewriter.

4:1e   Learn the Use of BAD and BADLY

After verbs that express actions of the senses, like *feel, look, smell, sound,* and *taste,* use the adjective *bad* rather than the adverb *badly*.

Incorrect: I **feel badly** about that.
Correct: I **feel bad** about that.

In all other cases, use the adverb *badly* to modify a verb or adjective.

Incorrect: They **need** help **bad**.
Correct: They **need** help **badly**.
Incorrect: That is a **bad behaved** child.
Correct: That is a **badly behaved** child.

4:1f   Learn the Use of GOOD and WELL

After verbs that express actions of the senses, like *feel, look, smell, sound,* and *taste,* use the adjective *good* rather than the adverb *well*.

Incorrect: The report **looks well**.
Correct: The report **looks good**.

In other cases use the adverb as usual to modify a verb or an adjective.

Incorrect: She **did good** the first day on the job.
Correct: She **did well** the first day on the job.

Exception: You say "You look well" when talking about someone's health, but you say "You look good" when you mean that someone's appearance is pleasing.

4:1g   Remember the Subjunctive (WAS and WERE)

When you are expressing a wish or a supposition, you use the subjunctive mood. The best example of this is the use of *was* and *were*. *Was* is in the indicative mood and is used to declare a fact: I *was* there at the time.

Were is in the subjunctive mood and is used to speculate: I wish I *were* there when it happened.

Here are some more instances of incorrect usage that you should guard against when describing conditions contrary to fact, highly improbable or wishful thinking:

Incorrect:	If I **was** rich I'd travel around the world.
Correct:	If I **were** rich I'd travel around the world.
Incorrect:	She acts as if she **was** the person in charge.
Correct:	She acts as if she **were** the person in charge.

4:1h   Be Careful with I and ME

Everyone knows that the following sentences should read:

- He gave the correspondence *to me*.

or
- I handled the correspondence *for him*.

Confusion can arise when the sentences are slightly more complicated.

Incorrect:	He dictated the correspondence to **Mary** and **I**.
Correct:	He dictated the correspondence to **Mary** and **me**.
Incorrect:	It **was me** who handled the correspondence.
Correct:	It **was I** who handled the correspondence.

Rule 1: Always use *me* after a preposition, no matter what words comes between the two. Some common prepositions are *to, from, by, for,* and *in.*

Rule 2: Always use *I* after the verb *to be.*

4.1i Understand the SELF Pronouns

The *self* pronouns, such as *myself, himself, yourself,* and *themselves,* have only two proper functions: intensive and reflexive. Intensive pronouns intensify or emphasize another noun or pronoun in the sentence. Reflexive pronouns reflect back on another noun or pronoun in the sentence.

Intensive: The mayor **herself** will be speaking at the meeting.
Reflexive: He drove the car **himself**.

The problem arises when you substitute a *self* pronoun for another noun or pronoun in the sentence.

Incorrect: John and **myself** will attend the meeting.
  Correct: John and **I** will attend the meeting.

4:1j Watch Out for WHO and WHOM

Who is used as the subject of a verb, while *whom* is used as the object of a verb or preposition. Sometimes the use is obvious:

- He is the official *to whom* I mailed the notice.
- She is the secretary *who works* for Mr. Jones.

The usage can become confusing when *who* or *whom* is separated from the verb of which it is the subject or object.

- *Whom* would you like to meet? (object)
- *Who* shall I say is calling? (subject)

Hint: Substitute the pronoun *him* or *her* (for *whom*) and *he* or *she* (for *who*) in the sentence. Whichever one sounds right is usually the correct choice.

4:2 A GUIDE TO CLARITY OF MEANING

When people don't say what they mean, it can cause all sorts of problems from broken appointments to the loss of important accounts. An omitted or misplaced word or phrase can convey an entirely different meaning from the one intended.

4:2a Sins of Omission

Omission of a word can cause unnecessary confusion.

Confusing: The secretary and treasurer resigned.

Are you talking about **one** officer of the company or **two**.

Clear: The secretary and **the** treasurer resigned.

Here is another appropriate example:

Confusing: Mr. Calhoun likes the word processing system better than his
secretary.

This could mean that Mr. Calhoun likes the system better than his
secretary does, or that Mr. Calhoun likes the system better than he
likes his secretary.

Clear: Mr. Calhoun likes the word processing system better than his
secretary **does**.

4:2b Misplaced Modifiers

Modifiers should be placed immediately before or after the words
they modify. If you change their positions, you could change the
meaning of the sentence.

Confusing: We sell at a discount **only** in our annex.
    Clear: We sell at a discount in our annex **only**.

The word *only* must be placed with particular care. Look at
how the meaning changes in the following examples:

- *Only* we sell at a discount in our annex.
- We *only* sell at a discount in our annex.
- We sell *only* at a discount in our annex.
- We sell at a discount in our *only* annex.

Confusing: We will return the contracts that we received in error **by registered mail.**

Clear: We will return **by registered mail** the contracts we received in error.

Confusing: I saw the new computer **getting off the elevator.**

Clear: **Getting off the elevator**, I saw the new computer.

The boldface phase modifies the word *I* and should be placed next to it. Otherwise, you give the impression that the computer is getting off the elevator.

You can make the sentence even clearer if you add the conjunction *while.*

Clearer: **While** getting off the elevator, I saw the new computer.

4:2c Ambiguous Modifiers

When you use a modifier between two words, both of which it could modify, the meaning of the sentence is obscured.

Confusing: A taxpayer who cheats **frequently** gets penalized.

Is the speaker talking about a taxpayer who cheats frequently, or one who frequently gets penalized?

Clear: A taxpayer who **frequently cheats** gets penalized.

or

A taxpayer who cheats gets **penalized frequently**.

4:3 MAKING THE RIGHT CONNECTIONS

A conjunction connects words and groups of words. There are two kinds of conjunctions: *coordinating (and, but, or, nor, for, so,* and *yet)* and *subordinating (although, if, when, than, that, though, since,* and *while).* As you can see in the following examples, **a** simple change of conjunctions gives entirely different meanings:

- I am going to eat lunch **and** go shopping.
- I am going to eat lunch, **then** go shopping.
- I am going to eat lunch **or** go shopping.

The first sentence expresses simple addition by the use of **and**. The second sentence expresses a time lapse by the use of **then**. The third sentence indicates a choice of alternatives by the use of **or**.

Choose your conjunctions carefully and do not limit yourself. Become familiar with the various conjunctions and their use so no one can mistake your meaning.

4:3a   15 Ways to Use Conjunctions

Suppose you were to tell your boss, "**When** I asked for an appointment for you with Mr. Haven, his secretary was not sure that he could make it."

It would be much more precise to say, "**Although** I asked for an appointment for you with Mr. Haven, his secretary was not sure that he could make it."

When simply means *at the time*, but *although* means *in spite of the fact that* and indicates more concern on your part.

The following list is a reminder of the uses of the various conjunctions. Learn to choose those that will help you express yourself most clearly.

1. Addition

To express an added thought or idea, use conjunctions such as **and, again, also, besides, both, finally, further, furthermore, in addition, likewise, moreover, too**.

Example: I have completed the contracts **in addition** to typing the enclosure letters.

---

2. Choice

To indicate a choice use **else, either/or, neither/nor, nor, or, otherwise**.

Example: I can **either** get out the correspondence **or** make these important phone calls.

---

3. Comparison

For making comparisons, use **as, than, as much as, more than**.

Example: I did not accomplish **as much as** I would have liked.

---

4. Concession

To concede something, use *admitting that, although, assuming that, even if, no matter how, of course, though*.

Example: I would not go, **even if** I had the chance.

---

5. Consequence

To indicate a consequence, use *accordingly, as a consequence, as a result, consequently, hence, in this way, so then, therefore, thus*.

Example: Mr. Jones gave me these instructions, **so** I will follow them.

---

6. Contrast

To show contrast, use conjunctions such as *and yet, but, however, in contrast, in spite of, nevertheless, nor, notwithstanding, on the contrary, still, unfortunately, whereas, yet*.

Example: She finished her work **in spite of** the interruptions.

---

7. Extent

To show extent, use conjunctions such as *as, according, as far as, more than, rather than, so*.

Example: I felt the heat today, **more than** at any other time this summer.

---

8. Emphasis

To repeat an idea in order to emphasize it, use *and assuredly, as I have said, certainly, in fact, in other words, undoubtedly*.

Example: This has been a very productive day; **in fact**, everything has gone unusually well.

---

9. Explanation

To explain something, use *because, for, for example, for instance, in particular, more specifically, specifically*.

Example: We should devise some new systems; **for instance**, a more efficient way of routing the mail would be helpful.

---

10. Location
To indicate location use **where** and **wherever**.

Example: Our salespeople travel **wherever** their territory requires.

---

11. Purpose
To indicate purpose use **in order that, that, why**.

Example: That is the reason **why** the salesperson is going to Rochester.

---

12. Reason
To indicate reason, use **as, because, for, since, whereas**.

Example: The salesperson is going to Rochester **since** that is part of his territory.

---

13. Supposition
To indicate supposition or condition, use **except, if, otherwise, provided, supposing, unless**.

Example: I'll leave early, **provided** I can get the time off.

---

14. Result
To indicate a result, use **because, of which, on account of which, so that, that is**.

Example: I have arranged my schedule **so that** I can have lunch at one o'clock.

---

15. Time
To indicate time, use **after, as, as long as, before, meanwhile, now that, since, until, when, whenever, while**.

Example: The workload will slacken **after** the holidays.

4:4   KEYS TO CORRECT SENTENCE STRUCTURE

A sentence that is clear, correct, and effective performs an important function in communication. You cannot stop to consider grammatical correctness every time you open your mouth to speak, but you can watch out for flaws and try to improve the errors in your speech.

4:4a   Unnecessary ANDS and BUTS

A common error in sentence structure is the insertion of **and** or **but** before the words **which** or **who**.

Incorrect: She is an intelligent woman, **and who** is an industrious worker.

This is a great typewriter, **and which** you will enjoy using.

He showed much enthusiasm at first, **but which** soon evaporated.

Correct: She is an intelligent woman, **who** is an industrious worker.

This is a great typewriter, **which** you will enjoy using.

He showed much enthusiasm at first, **which** soon evaporated.

4:4b   AS and LIKE

Do not use **as** as a substitute for **whether** or **that**.

Incorrect: She was not sure **as** she could go to the party.
Correct: She was not sure **whether** (or **that**) she could go to the party.

Although **like** is often used in casual conversation and in advertising as a substitute for **as, as if**, or **as though**, it is not correct.

Incorrect: I feel **like** I should stay late tonight.
Correct: I feel **that** I should stay late tonight.
Incorrect: The movie seemed **like** it would never end.
Correct: The movie seemed **as if** (or **as though**) it would never end.

4:4c   IS, WHERE, IS WHEN, IS BECAUSE

Do not use the adverbial clauses **is where, is when, is because** in place of a noun or a noun phrase.

Incorrect:	Indexing **is where** you arrange files in alphabetical or numerical order.
Correct:	Indexing **is the arrangement** of files in alphabetical or numerical order.
Incorrect:	Follow-up **is when** you file material so it will be brought to someone's attention at a certain date.
Correct:	Follow-up **is a method** of filing material so it will be brought to someone's attention at a certain date.

When you begin a thought with "The reason is" or "The reason was," follow it with a noun or noun clause introduced by *that*. The use of *the reason was because* is redundant.

Incorrect:	I couldn't go to the show; **the reason was because** I had to work late.
Correct:	I couldn't go to the show **because** I had to work late.

or

The **reason** I couldn't go to the show was **that** I had to work late.

4:4d The Split Infinitive

The infinitive is the "to + verb" form: *to go, to understand*. Ordinarily, the infinitive should be kept intact, but the split infinitive is not considered a major fault, and it is sometimes necessary in order to keep your meaning clear. Whether to split or not to split depends on whether the sentence sounds awkward or the meaning is distorted.

Split and Awkward:	He asked me **to immediately write** the letter.
Clear:	He asked me **to write** the letter **immediately**.
Split but Clear:	I've scheduled your appointment **to just precede** the meeting.
Confusing:	I've scheduled your appointment **just to precede** the meeting.
Impossible:	I've scheduled your appointment **to precede just** the meeting.

4:4e The Terminal Preposition

The original reason for the rule about never ending a sentence with a preposition was that a sentence should never be ended with a weak word. While this rule is observed to some extent in written sentences, it is usually overlooked in spoken language. Here again, grammatical correctness must sometimes give way to the possibility of awkwardness or confusion. For example, the following sentence is more proper when it ends with a noun, but it sounds more natural with the preposition at the end.

Written: We have no material on hand **with** which to fill your order.
Spoken: We have no material on hand to fill your order **with**.

A question also sounds better when it ends with a preposition.

Awkward: **For** what are you waiting?
Clear: What are you waiting **for**?

Sometimes there is no other way to end a sentence except with a preposition: The speaker was jeered *at*.

4:5 ACHIEVING SENTENCE COORDINATION

Sentence coordination means using similar constructions to express similar ideas.

Awkward: She likes **to read** and **playing** the stereo.
Improved: She likes **to read** and **to play** the stereo.
or
She likes **reading** and **playing** the stereo.

4:5a Parallelism

The technical term for sentence coordination is ***parallelism***. This involves matching phrases, clauses, and active or passive verbs so that they are constructed from the same grammatical forms. Using parallelism improves sentence clarity.

Awkward:	Betty is a secretary **with great potential** and **who wants** to learn the business.
Clear:	Betty is a secretary **who has** great potential and **who wants** to learn the business.

or

Betty is a secretary with great potential who wants to learn the business.

Awkward:	She bought a dress **with a pleated skirt** and **having a cowl neckline.**
Clear:	She bought a dress **with a pleated skirt** and (with) **a cowl neckline.** (The word **with** does not need to be repeated, as it is understood.)

4:5b Parallelism in a Series

When you are describing something in a series of three, *make sure that the sentence elements are in parallel form.*

Awkward:	The play was **exciting, colorful, and had a good cast.**
Clear:	The play was **exciting, colorful, and well-cast.**

4:5c Parallelism in Lists

Treat items in a list or outline as you would items in a series, since they belong together.

Awkward:	The word processing software has the following capabilities:
	• will perform word wraps
	• can do search and locate functions
	• cutting and pasting
	• create an index
Clear:	The word processing software has the following capabilities:
	• will perform word wraps
	• can do search and locate functions
	• can cut and paste
	• can create an index

4:5d Consistency in Parallelism

Words used in parallel structure must be the same parts of speech and must stand for comparable ideas.

Awkward: Mr. Lawrence's assistant is **good-looking** and has a fine **education**.

Clear: Mr. Lawrence's assistant is **good-looking** and **well-educated**.

Awkward: Ms. Martin thinks her **work** is more important than the **bookkeeper**.

Clear: Ms Martin thinks her **work** is more important than **that of the bookkeeper**.

or

Ms. Martin thinks her **work** is more important than the work of the bookkeeper.

4:5e Misleading Parallelism

Parallel structure should not be used for sentence elements which are unequal in kind or importance.

Awkward: **For his sake, for a sandwich and a cup of coffee,** I will help him.

Clear: **For his sake,** I will help him **with a sandwich and a cup of coffee.**

Awkward: **They went** to the conference and **they had a** rented limousine

Clear: **They went** to the conference **in a** rented limousine.

4:6 ELIMINATING SUPERFLUOUS WORDS

Many people use language that is grammatically correct but tiresome. They overload their sentences with unnecessary words and phrases that cause their listeners' attention to wander. This is particularly unfortunate in business conversation, where getting to the point quickly should be the objective.

4:6a The Fact That

The expression *the fact that* can usually be replaced with something more direct.

Wordy:	**Owing to the fact that** the shipment was delayed, we could not keep the delivery date.
Direct:	**Because** the shipment was delayed, we could not keep the delivery date.
Wordy:	**In spite of the fact that** we are shorthanded, we expect to complete the job on time.
Direct:	**Although** we are shorthanded, we expect to complete the job on time.
Wordy:	Let me **call your attention to the fact that** payment is a month overdue.
Direct:	Let me **remind you** that payment is a month overdue.

4:6b   Other Expressions to Avoid

Avoid	Use
along the lines of	like
blue in color	blue
consequently	so
come in contact with	meet
different in character	different
during the time that	while
for the purpose of	to
for the reason that	since, because
furthermore	then
in many cases	often
in a hasty manner	hastily
in the event of	if
in the nature of	like, similar to
likewise	and
one and the same	the same
seems evident that	seems that
six in number	six
there is no doubt but that	no doubt
with the result that	so that

CHART I: PRONUNCIATION REMINDER

Here is a list of commonly mispronounced words with the preferred pronunciation for each (some have alternate acceptable pronunciations). You can make your own chart of words you mispronounce, along with the correct pronunciation of each. You may also want to add words from the lists given in chapter 1.

Adjectives

chic	SHEEK
genuine	GEN-yoo-inn
miniature	MIN-ee-uh-choor
robust	ro-BUST
sacrilegious	sak-ruh-LIH-jus

Nouns

accessory	ak-SES-eh-ree
experiment	ek-SPEHR-uh-ment
italics	ih-TAL-iks
radiator	RAY-dee-ay-tur
theater	THEE-uh-tur

Verbs

hypnotize	HIP-neh-tize
menstruate	MEN-stroo-ate
plagiarize	PLAY-juh-rize
route	ROOT
surprise	surr-PRIZE

CHART II: SYNONYMS TO REMEMBER

Instead of using the same descriptive words all the time, vary your speech occasionally with an appropriate synonym. Make your own list of words you use frequently, along with synonyms for alternate uses, but always check the meaning of the synonym to make sure that it fits your purpose. Remember that the object of this list is not to inflate your vocabulary but to give it some variety.

Instead Of	Sometimes Use
bright	brilliant
difficult	arduous
example	sample
execute	administer
fear	apprehension
grief	anguish
happy	jovial
knowledge	erudition
large	gigantic
mysterious	inscrutable
necessary	essential
obscure	abstruse
perceive	comprehend
question	inquiry
rare	unique
miscellaneous	motley
sad	dejected
usual	habitual

PART II

EFFECTIVE WRITING

5

Grammar Simplified

There is only one genuine rule of grammar: There are no hard and fast rules. Any construction that is used often enough and widely enough automatically becomes right and proper. Nevertheless, there are certain principles that should be observed. Brushing up on the ones described in this chapter should help refresh your memory and improve your skills in writing and typing letters and memos. But before you can get to the business of subject, verb, and pronoun agreement and other such matters of grammar, you probably need a quick refresher on the basic parts of speech.

5:1 EIGHT PARTS OF SPEECH AND HOW TO USE THEM

Words are divided into parts of speech according to their form, function, and meaning. These parts include (1) nouns, (2) pronouns, (3) verbs, (4) adjectives, (5) adverbs, (6) conjunctions, (7) prepositions, and (8) interjections. For the sake of simplicity, they are categorized into five groups with an extra category called "hybrids."

Nouns and Pronouns: words that name

Adjectives and Adverbs: words that modify

Prepositions and Conjunctions: words that connect

Interjections: words that exclaim

Verbs: words that show action or state of being

Hybrids: words that can function in more than one capacity

5:1a   Nouns and Pronouns

A noun names a person (*Jane*), place (*Los Angeles*), or thing (*telephone*). A noun can also represent a quality (*beauty*), idea (*dream*), or action (*speed*). A noun can be distinguished by its position in a sentence as a subject before the verb, and object after the verb, and an object of a preposition. It can also be used as a modifier with the addition of *'s*.

Subject:	The **invoice** was mailed yesterday.
Object:	I mailed you the **invoice** yesterday. I attached the invoice to my letter.
Modifier:	The **book's** cover was damaged in transit.
	Mr. Jones's records are in the file.

Pronouns are words that are used in place of nouns. They consist of the following groups:

Demonstrative:	this, that, these, those
Relative:	who, whom, which, what, that, whose, (**which** and **that** refer to things; **who** and **whom** refer to people.)
Interrogative:	who? which? what? whom? whose?
Personal:	I, you, we, he, she, it, they, me, us, him, his, her, their
Indefinite:	everybody, some, anyone, someone, no one, each, none
Intensive/Reflexive:	myself, himself, herself, yourself, itself, ourselves, yourselves, themselves

Personal pronouns are one of the toughest problems in English for the average person. Confusion often arises over the use of pronoun *case*, the form that shows its function in the sentence. Most pronouns have three different case forms: *nominative* or *subjective* (used as a subject), *objective* (used as an object), and *possessive* (showing possession). Take the following test. The answers are at the end of this chapter.

Personal Pronoun Test

1. She can complete the job faster than (I, me).
2. I do not have as much authority as (he, him).
3. It was a confidential matter between you and (she, her).
4. Everyone was present except (they, them).
5. No one besides (he, him) had any difficulty passing the test.
6. We have considered everyone else for the position except (she, her).
7. The two who worked on Saturday were John and (I, me).
8. You are ahead of Ruth and (I, me) in seniority.
9. What would the company do without (we, us) secretaries?
10. (We, Us) secretaries are indispensable.
11. Each department has (its it's) own system.
12. The final choice is (yours, your's).

Tips for the Correct Answers

1. After **as** and **than**, finish the sentence by supplying the verb to help choose the correct pronoun.
2. After prepositions, use the objective form of the pronoun: **me, him, her, us**, and **them.**
3. After any form of the verb **to be**, use the nominative form of the pronoun: **I, he, she, we**, and **they.**
4. When you have a double form pronoun/noun combination, use the pronoun alone and the answer will be obvious: We (secretaries) are indispensable.
5. When a pronoun is the subject of a sentence, use the nominative form.
6. Personal pronouns form the possessive by adding **s.**

5:1b Adjectives and Adverbs

An adjective modifies a noun or pronoun and makes its meaning more exact. There are three general types of adjectives: *descriptive, limiting*, and *proper*.

Descriptive: a **red** hat, a **hard** task, a **broken** pen

Limiting: the **seventh** day, our **former** address, **several** choices, **that** book

Proper: the **British** rights, an **Italian** import

Many descriptive adjectives change their forms to indicate degree: *good, better, best*. A common problem in the use of adjectives is the confusion of the comparative with the superlative degree in sentences like these:

Incorrect: I paid the **largest** of the two bills.
Correct: I paid the **larger** of the two bills.

Most adjectives end in **er** for the comparative degree and in **est** for the superlative. The comparative degree refers to two persons or things. The superlative refers to more than two.

Incorrect: I have tried all of the machines and this one is **easier** to handle.
Correct: I have tried all of the machines and this one is **easiest** to handle.

Some adjectives do not lend themselves to the **er** and **est** endings, in which case they are combined with **more** or **most**.

• I wish you would be **more cautious**.
• She was the **most qualified** applicant.

Adverbs modify verbs, adjectives, or other adverbs. In the following instances, **almost, very**, and **faintly** are the adverbs:

Verb: The telephone bell **rang faintly**.
Adjective: We are **almost ready** to open.
Adverb: We can guarantee **very fast** delivery.

One way in which adverbs can be distinguished from corresponding adjectives is that many adverbs end in **ly**.

Adjective	Adverb
bad	badly
sure	surely
easy	easily
neat	neatly
temporary	temporarily

Another method of discovering whether a word is an adverb is to ask the questions, "When?" "Where?" "How?" and "How much?" Words that answer any of these questions will almost always be adverbs.

When?	now, early, late, yesterday
Where?	here, there, above, below, far, near
How?	rapidly, slowly, badly
How Much?	often, seldom, partly, entirely

Some adverbs are compared by the addition of **more** or **most**, while others are compared by the endings **er** and **est**.

- She typed the contracts **more rapidly** than I did.
- This is the form we use **most often**.
- Our busy season is drawing near**er**.
- The near**est** airport is Kennedy.

5:1c Prepositions and Conjunctions

A preposition links a noun or pronoun with another word in the sentence.

- We expect to have the proposal ready **by** Friday.
- We called you **on** the thirtieth.
- You will hear **from** me soon.

Other commonly used prepositions are **against, among, around, at, before, behind, below, between, beyond, during, for, in, like, of, since, to, until, with**.

Prepositions are often used in idiomatic phrases:

comply with	different from
adapted to	listen to
angry with	wait for
fond of	independent of
with regard to	according to

Prepositions should not be omitted when needed for clarity.

Unclear:	He will call you September 15.
Clear:	He will call you **on** September 15.

> **Unclear:** She was not aware nor responsible for the problem.
> **Clear:** She was not aware **of** nor responsible for the problem.

Conjunctions join words or groups of words in a sentence. When they join elements of equal grammatical rank, they are called **coordinating.** Your choice of a conjunction depends on the exact meaning you want to convey.

Meaning	Conjunction
Addition	and, both, also, too, further
Choice	either, or, neither, nor, else, otherwise
Contrast	but, yet, still, notwithstanding, however
Consequence	therefore, then, so, hence, consequently

> **Addition:** The contract **and** the check are enclosed.
> **Choice:** **Neither** the contract **nor** the check was enclosed.
> **Contrast:** The contract was enclosed **but** the check was not.
> **Consequence:** The contract has been signed, **so** I am returning it to you.

Subordinating conjunctions join dependent clauses to main clauses. Subordinating conjunctions can be grouped according to the meaning of the sentence.

Meaning	Conjunction
Time	as, while, until, before, since, after
Reason	as, whereas, because, for, since
Condition	if, unless, except, otherwise
Comparison	as, according, as far as, so

> **Time:** Mr. Atkins will arrive **before** the convention begins.
> **Reason:** We are moving **because** our lease has expired.
> **Condition:** We shall have to foreclose **if** we do not hear from you by the first of the month.
> **Comparison:** Mr. Atkins will be free all morning, **as far as** I know.

5:1d   Interjections

An **interjection** is a word used for exclamation. It can be followed by a comma or an exclamation point, depending on the amount of emphasis to be placed on the word. Although you won't find much use for interjections in business writing, you should recognize the common ones like *oh, my, indeed,* and *wow*.

- *Wow*! That was a long meeting.
- *Oh*, I think I'll work through lunch today.

5:1e Verbs

A verb shows action or state of being. Verbs can be classified by *principal parts (infinitive* or *present, past, past participle)* from which the tenses are formed, by type (*transitive* or *intransitive*), by *mood, (indicative, imperative, subjunctive)*, and by *voice (active, passive)*.

Active voice means that the subject performs the action. *Passive* voice means that the subject receives the action. Sentences in active voice always have a stronger effect.

Active:	We **wrote** the letter yesterday.
Passive:	The letter **was written** yesterday.
Active:	He **asked** us to reply.
Passive:	We **were asked** to reply.

There are four ways to identify the verb in a sentence. The verb is the word that denotes an action, a happening, a fulfillment, or a condition.

Action:	The stock market **crashed.**
	Get moving! (The subject **you** is understood.)
Happening:	It **occurred** in 1929.
Fulfillment:	We **have succeeded** in our attempts to find a new formula.
Condition:	Prices **are** rising.

See how many verbs you can recognize in the following test:

Verb Recognition Test

Dear Mr. Yates:

We hope you have set aside the week of May 14 in order to attend the Dealers Convention to be held in Atlanta this year.

The seminars will be held at the Peachtree Plaza Hotel, and sessions will start each morning at nine o'clock in the Peachtree Room. Lunch will be served in the Georgian Ballroom from twelve until two. After two, you are free for relaxation, and evening entertainment has been arranged.

The cost of the entire week, including transportation by Delta Airlines from Boston to Atlanta, will be $1450. The plane will leave Logan International Airport on May 14 at 8 A.M. To reserve your space, please fill in the attached reservation form and return it to us. No reservations will be accepted after May 1.

We know you will find your stay enjoyable as well as productive, and we look forward to your participation.

Sincerely,

How many verbs were you able to identify? Eighteen would be perfect, fifteen would be good, and a score of below fifteen shows that you may have trouble identifying verbs. (The answers are at the end of this chapter.)

5:1f Hybrids

Some words become different parts of speech according to the way they are used. When verbs become nouns they are called **gerunds** and they are used exactly like nouns. They always end in **ing** and are often preceded by possessive nouns.

- Her **going** to lunch early was inconvenient.
- His **writing** the letter saved a phone call.
- **Smoking** is not permitted in the dining room.

Nouns become adjectives when they are used as possessives.

- The **executives'** washroom
- The **ladies'** lounge

Nouns are sometimes used as adjectives without the addition of **'s** or **s'**.

- The item comes in four **decorator** colors.
- We have a complete line of **designer** sportswear.

Certain nouns and verbs are used interchangeably, and the only way to tell which part of speech they are is by the way they are used.

- I think we will be able to **effect** a settlement. (verb)
- We are feeling the **effect** of the recession. (noun)

(See **affect** and **effect** on page 92.)

5:2   TWO SIMPLE PRINCIPLES

Now that you have reviewed the parts of speech and their function in a sentence, you're ready to reacquaint yourself with two simple principles to make your letters and memos grammatically correct.

5:2a   Agreement of Subject and Verb

In the following sentences, it is obvious that the singular subject takes a singular verb, and the plural subject takes a plural verb.

- **Mary has** a headache.
- Her **headaches have become** chronic.

Not all sentences are as simple and obvious as these, however. Here are a few samples of more complex constructions that may cause confusion.

1. Alternative Subjects
Alternative subjects are usually separated by **or** or **nor**, and the verb takes its number from the subject nearest to it.

- Neither the chart nor the **graphs are** suitable for our use.
- Neither the graphs nor the **chart is** suitable for our use.

2. Collective Nouns
A collective noun, like **board** or **committee**, is generally considered singular and takes a singular verb.

- The **board has** decided to postpone action on the measure.

3. Compound Subject

Two or more subjects joined by **and** take a plural verb.

• Mr. Jones **and** Mr. Kane **are** out of town.

4. Separation of Subject and Verb

The verb must agree with the subject, in spite of any separation by an intervening expression (**along with, including, in addition to, together with, as well as,** and similar expressions) or a prepositional phrase.

• The **President**, along with his aides and staff, **is** arriving tomorrow.
• A **catalog** of office furnishings and supplies **is** available.

5. Relative Pronoun Used as a Subject

When a relative pronoun (**who, which, that**) is used as the subject of a clause, the verb agrees with the noun or other pronoun that the relative pronoun refers to (its antecedent).

• The meeting is one of **those that are** scheduled for Wednesday mornings.
• Polio is among those **diseases that have** a vaccine for prevention.

6. Subject That Follows the Verb

When the subject follows the verb, the verb still agrees with the subject in number.

• In this type of desk **are** three convenient **drawers**.

7. Subject and Linking Verb

A linking verb (**is, are, was**) agrees with the subject, not with the subject complement (predicate nominative).

• The **error** in your order **is** the measurements.
• Production **costs are** the cause of the price increase.

8. Singular Subjects Plural in Form

Subjects like **economics, news,** and **politics,** which are plural in form (end in **s**) but singular in meaning, take singular verbs.

- Today the *news is* good.
- The *economics* of the situation *is* in question.

9. Singular Pronouns

Singular pronouns take singular verbs, even when a phrase intervenes.

- *Everybody is* going to be there.
- *Each* of us *has* contributed to the fund.
- *Someone* always *meets* visitors at the airport.
- *One* of them *is* responsible.

10. Quantities or Numbers

A subject that is plural in form, but which indicates a quantity or number, takes a singular verb when the subject is a unit in itself.

- *Twenty-five dollars is* too much to ask.
- *Three quarts is* sufficient.

5:2b   Agreement of Pronoun and Antecedent

A pronoun always agrees, in all respects, with the word for which it stands (its antecedent).

1. A pronoun always agrees *in number* with the word for which it stands.

- A *man* should remove *his* hat in the elevator.
- *Men* should remove *their* hats in the elevator.

2. *Everyone* and *everybody* are singular pronouns and should take singular pronouns to refer to them.

- *Everyone* is going to wear *her* formal dress to the Christmas party.

3. A pronoun agrees with the nearer of two antecedents.

- Neither the desk nor the filing *cabinets* are up to *their* usual standard.
- Neither the filing cabinets nor the *desk* is up to *its* usual standard.

4. A collective noun takes either a singular or plural pronoun, depending on the meaning of the antecedent in the sentence. Here the word **committee** is considered as a unit:

- The **committee** decided to continue **its** discussions.

Here the members are acting individually:

- The **committee** took a break to return to their offices.

5:3   SEXIST LANGUAGE AND HOW TO AVOID IT

In the history of the English language, the masculine pronoun **he** was intended to stand for both sexes. Until fairly recently, such usage posed little problem in business since the lines were clear between the sexes. Men were chairmen and executives; women were secretaries and clerks. Now, of course, it is common for women to be executives and men to be secretaries, and language is changing to reflect this.

5:3a   Correct Choice of Gender

A pronoun should always agree in gender (masculine or feminine) with the word for which it stands. It was once acceptable to write the following:

- A secretary should not leave her telephone unattended.
- An executive is expected to be at his desk promptly in the morning.

Such writing would now be considered sexist, however, because a secretary could be a man and an executive could be a woman.
     Likewise, the following sentence is sexist:

- Everyone is expected to improve his performance.

The masculine pronoun is no longer adequate to refer to both sexes.

5:3b   Ways to Avoid Problems with Choice of Gender

Use the plural form whenever possible. Plural nouns require plural pronouns, and the plural pronoun **their** is neither masculine nor feminine.

- Secretaries should not leave *their* telephones unattended.
- Executives are expected to be at *their* desks promptly in the morning.

Use the articles (*a, an, the*) whenever possible in place of the gender-specific pronouns (*his, her*).

- *A* secretary should not leave *the* telephone unattended.
- *An* executive is expected to be at *the* office promptly in the morning.
- *A* secretary should submit *an* attendance card at the end of every week.

If such a construction isn't possible, use both pronouns (*his and her* or *her and his*).

- A secretary should not leave *her or his* telephone unattended.

In other cases, you may be able to revise the sentence without changing the meaning. For example,

- The executive should make up his mind about pay raises for his staff.

could be changed to

- The executive should decide about pay raises for the staff.

Change singular indefinite pronouns (*everybody, everyone, anybody,* etc.) to the plural whenever possible:

- All secretaries are expected to improve their performance.

Avoid the following construction, which is common in spoken English but is grammatically incorrect:

- Everybody is expected to improve their performance.

5:3c Nonsexist Substitutes for Sexist Language

It's easy to avoid sexist language if you become aware of the hidden message it sends and learn to use the recommended substitutes.

Sexist	Nonsexist
mankind	humanity, human beings, human race, people
man	person
manhours	work hours
man-made	artificial, synthetic
manpower	human energy, workers, work force
businessman	businessperson, business executive
salesman	sales representative, salesperson
insurance man	insurance agent
chairman	chair, chairperson, head
draftsman	drafter
foreman	supervisor
workman	worker

5:3d Job Titles That Have Changed to Eliminate Sexist Language

Numerous job titles have been changed to avoid sexism. A partial list follows.

Former Job Title	Current Job Title
mailman	post worker, mail carrier
stewardess, air hostess, steward	flight attendant
garbage man	sanitation worker
policeman	police officer
congressman	member of Congress

It is unnecessary to add gender to titles, as in **male nurse** or **female doctor**. The terms are neither masculine nor feminine and need no clarification.

5:4 SIX BASIC TENSES OF VERBS

There are six basic verb tenses to indicate the three divisions of time: past, present, and future.

Present Tense
This tense indicates that the action or condition is going on, or exists, now.

- We *know* you will find your stay enjoyable as well as productive, and we *look* forward to seeing you.

Past Tense

The past tense indicates that the action or condition took place, or existed, at some definite time in the past.

- We hope you *found* your stay enjoyable as well as productive.

Future Tense

This tense is an indication that the action or condition will take place, or exist, sometime in the future.

- The seminars *will be held* at the Peachtree Plaza Hotel and sessions *will start* each morning at nine.

Present Perfect Tense

The present perfect tense indicates an action or condition begun in the past and continued or completed in the present.

- After two, you are free for relaxation, and evening entertainment *has been arranged*.

Past Perfect Tense

This tense indicates an action or condition completed in the past before another past action.

- We found that evening entertainment *had been arranged*.

Future Perfect Tense

This tense indicates that an action or condition will be completed or will exist before a specific time in the future.

- The first seminar *will have concluded* before you arrive.

Most people learn to use the appropriate tenses when they are children, long before they know the names that grammarians have given them. The tense that is a bit tricky is the future perfect. Be careful not to omit the *have*.

Incorrect: On Monday, he will be gone for two weeks.

Correct: On Monday, he will **have** been gone for two weeks.

5:5 THOSE DECEPTIVE SOUND-ALIKE WORDS

In English there are a number of words that sound so much alike that you may be tempted to use one for the other. Be careful of this, for the meanings are usually quite different.

accept	to receive
except	to exclude
ad	abbreviation of **advertisement**
add	to make an addition
adapt	to adjust
adopt	to accept
advice	counsel (noun)
advise	to counsel or notify (verb)
affect	to influence or to pretend
effect	to bring about (verb)
	result (noun)
all ready	prepared
already	by this time
altogether	entirely
all together	all of us or all of you
appraise	to estimate
apprise	to notify
ascent	the act of rising
assent	consent
biannual	twice a year
biennial	once in two years
bloc	a group
block	to stop
canvas	coarse cloth
canvass	to solicit
capital	a city
capitol	a building
cite	to quote
site	location

communicable	able to be transmitted
communicative	willing to convey ideas
compliment	an expression of admiration
complement	complete
consul	an official
council	an advisory group
counsel	advice
continual	often repeated
continuous	uninterrupted
credible	believable
credulous	easily convinced
creditable	worthy of praise
deprecate	to show disapproval
depreciate	to lower in value
dialect	regional speech
dialogue	conversation between two or more parties
disinterested	impartial
uninterested	lacking interest
emigrate	to leave a country or locality
immigrate	to enter a country or locality
every one	each one (followed by *of*)
everyone	all
farther	refers to distance
further	refers to time, quantity, or degree
formally	in a formal way
formerly	previously
guarantee	to promise or to secure (verb) something that assures a particular outcome (noun)
guaranty	a pledge of performance
healthful	giving health
healthy	having health
in	denotes location
into	movement from without to within
in to	indicates direction
lay	to set down or deposit something
lie	to recline or rest
lay	past tense of *lie*

limit	a boundary
limitation	a restriction
meanwhile	during an intervening time (adverb)
meantime	an interval (noun)
moral	proper or good
morale	the attitude of a group
official	holding a position of authority
officious	offering unwanted advice
persecute	to harass
prosecute	to bring legal proceedings
personal	private
personnel	a group of employees
practical	worth being put into practice
practicable	capable of being put into practice, but not always worthwhile
precede	to come before
proceed	to carry out
prescription	an order for dispensing medicine
proscription	a prohibition
principal	chief, main (adjective)
	the leader (noun)
	a sum of money (noun)
principle	a basic law or fact
somebody	an unspecified person
someone	some person
some one	a particular person
sometime	on some occasion
some time	a span of time
stationary	in a fixed position
stationery	writing paper and envelopes
stricture	severe criticism
structure	something constructed
their	possessive pronoun
there	at a certain place
they're	contraction of **they are**
vice	a defect or bad habit
vise	a clamp
waive	to give up
wave	a swell of water, a greeting with the hand

ANSWERS TO TESTS

Personal Pronoun Test

1. I	**7.** I
2. he	**8.** me
3. her	**9.** us
4. them	**10.** we
5. him	**11.** its
6. her	**12.** yours

Verb Recognition Test

First Paragraph

hope
have set
to attend
to be held

Second Paragraph

will be held
will start
will be served
to reserve
has been arranged

Third Paragraph

will be
will leave
are
fill in
return
will be accepted

Fourth Paragraph

know
will find
look

6

Quick and Easy Punctuation

Punctuation was not invented until the fifteenth century, but the twentieth-century secretary cannot function without it. You can judge whether you are using punctuation correctly by rereading a letter you have just written. If you get out of breath before the end of a sentence, you have probably used too little punctuation. If the effect is halting and uneven, perhaps you used too many commas—a common mistake.

6:1: SECRETS OF COMMA PLACEMENT

Commas usually indicate the normal breathing places in a sentence. Because they show the reader where to take a short pause, they clarify the meaning of the sentence. Comma usage falls into four general categories.

6:1a Rule of Three

In a series of three or more items with a single conjunction, use a comma after each item preceding the conjunction.

- I opened the letter, read it, and informed Mr. Ames of its contents.
- We interview applicants on Mondays, Wednesdays, and Fridays.

Exception: Contemporary usage has made the last comma in a series optional if the meaning is clear without it.

- The supply clerk ordered computer paper, printer ribbons and bond for the new department head.

If it is obvious that three distinct items were ordered, the comma can be omitted. However, many grammarians still recommend adding the last comma before the conjunction since it makes clear the exact number of items in the series.

For business firms containing names in a series, follow their example for correct comma usage, which will be indicated in their letterhead and any other printed matter.

6:1b   With Nonessential Phrases

A nonessential phrase can be omitted without changing the meaning of the sentence. The phrase provides interesting or useful, but not essential, information. In such cases, two commas are required—one before and one after the phrase—to set it off from the rest of the sentence.

- Mr. Albert Baynes, **whom you met last summer**, has been appointed head of the committee.

The sentence would still make sense without the section enclosed by commas.

6:1c   Before BUT, AND, OR, FOR, and NOR

Place a comma before **and, but, for, or,** and **nor** (the coordinating conjunctions) when they join two independent clauses, unless the clauses are very short.

- We received your letter, **but** the merchandise has not yet arrived.
- I am glad you called the matter to my attention, **for** it is my job to serve you.
- The meeting is important, **and** I plan to attend.

6:1d   After Introductory Words, Phrases, and Clauses

Place a comma after introductory words, phrases, and clauses, those elements that come before the subject and verb of the sentence.

- After studying the problem, I determined that it can be solved.
- Because of the shortage of help we've been experiencing, we have not finished this job on time.
- Yes, I'd be happy to do that for you.

Exception: When the introductory phrase or clause is short, the comma can be omitted if it does not cause any confusion.

- In these cases I follow a special procedure.

6:1e Within Dates and Addresses

In a date consisting of the month, the day, and the year, set off the year by commas. Omit the commas in a date consisting of only the month and the year.

- Our company was founded by John Bates on April 25, 1932.
- Our company was founded by John Bates in April 1932.

In an address, use a comma to separate each element from the rest of the sentence.

- Atlanta, Georgia, is my home.
- The letter was addressed to Ms. Mary Johnson, 604 Spring Street, Olivette, MO 63132.

Note: No comma separates the zip code from the state.

6:1f With Numbers

In numbers containing four or more figures, use a comma between every group of three figures, counting from the right.

> 3,987
> 39,870
> 398,705
> 3,987,050

6:1g Before and After Quotation

Use commas before and after quotations that are incorporated into the sentence. (See also 6:8b.)

- The speaker said, "We must increase production if we want to increase profits."
- "We must increase production," the speaker said, "if we want to increase profits."
- "We must increase production," the speaker said.

Inside or Outside? The rule of comma placement has no exceptions in American usage. The comma is *always* placed *inside* quotation marks.

6:1h Guarding Against Four Common Errors

Here are some cautions for the secretary who may be tempted to use too many commas.

1. Do not use a comma to separate a subject from its verb or a verb from its object.

Incorrect: Members with charge cards, can be billed for purchases.
The product we are featuring, is called Zanadu.

Correct: Members with charge cards can be billed for purchases.
The product we are featuring is called Zanadu.

---

2. Do not use a comma *after* a conjunction like *but* or *and*. The comma goes *before* the conjunction.

Incorrect: We like your idea **but**, the consensus is that it would not work for us.

Correct: We like your idea, **but** the consensus is that it would not work for us.

---

3. Do not use a comma to separate two words or phrases joined by *and, but, or, nor,* or *for.*

Incorrect: She has ability, **and** integrity. (**And** connects two nouns—**ability** and **integrity**.)
I went to the post office, **but** forgot to get your package. (**But** connects two verbs—**went** and **forgot**).

Correct: She has ability and integrity.
I went to the post office but forgot to get your package.

Exception: A comma is sometimes needed to make your meaning perfectly clear, even when the rule says otherwise.

- For as little as twenty-five dollars you can buy a complete makeup kit, or a one-ounce bottle of perfume and a four-ounce container of spray cologne.

The comma before the perfume and spray items indicates that they go together.

Introductory clauses should always be followed by a comma to avoid confusion.

- Whenever practicable, action should be taken to facilitate speedier delivery.

4. Do no use commas to separate essential phrases and clauses from the rest of the sentence. The most common errors involve clauses beginning with *that*.

Incorrect: The typewriter, **that** I have been using for five years, is too old for repair.

He is not permitted to eat food, **that** contains high levels of cholesterol.

Correct: The typewriter **that** I have been using for five years is too old for repair.

He is not permitted to eat food **that** contains high levels of cholesterol.

6:2 WHERE TO USE THE SEMICOLON

The semicolon indicates a division that is more emphatic than a comma but not as forceful as a period. It has four distinct uses.

6:2a To Separate Related Clauses

When related clauses are not separated by a conjunction, use a semicolon instead.

- Please remit at once; the bill is long overdue.

When related clauses are lengthy, even if they are separated by a conjunction, use a semicolon, especially if the clauses already contain commas.

- The first job we have open involves typing letters, memos, and reports; and the second requires some familiarity with legal documents, court papers, and legal citations.

6:2b   To Separate Listed Items

Place semicolons between elements in a series if they are long or are already punctuated by commas.

- We have branches in Albany, New York; Hartford, Connecticut; and Springfield, Massachusetts.
- We interview applicants on the third Monday of every month from ten to twelve; on alternate Wednesdays from one to three; and all day Friday, except on the Friday before a holiday.

6:2c   Before Conjunctive Adverbs

Use a semicolon before an adverb that acts as a conjunction (conjunctive adverb) such as *accordingly, also, besides, consequently, however, nevertheless, otherwise,* and *therefore*.

- You placed your order soon enough; *however*, an unexpected shortage has caused a delay.
- We were pleased with the samples you sent; *therefore*, we would like to place an order.

6:2d   Before Transitional Phrases

Use a semicolon to separate two clauses when the second clause begins with a transitional phrase like *as a result, after all, for example,* or *that is*.

- We would like to hear from you in greater detail regarding your background; *that is*, send a résumé of your education, experience, and salary expectations.
- Our office has flexible hours; as a result, we have coverage from 8 A.M. to 7 P.M.

6:3   THE PERIOD

The period has three uses, none of which is very complicated.

1. At the end of a declarative or imperative sentence:

- Your suggestions were very helpful. (declarative)
- Do not proceed until you hear from us. (imperative)

2. After initials and abbreviations, except those used as symbols, like CBS, CIA, or two-letter state abbreviations, like CA, IL, and NY.

Ms.

D.D.S.

a.m.

E.S.T.

Jr.

3. After each letter or number in an outline or list, unless the letter or number is enclosed in parentheses. Do not use a period after 1st, 2nd, or 3rd, or similar contractions.

3.

IV.

(5)

6th

6:3a   When to Omit a Period

1. After an abbreviation, omit a second period when the abbreviation comes at the end of a sentence.

- He was defeated in the election by John Johnson, Jr.

2. After sums of money in dollar denominations, omit the period unless cents are added.

- I enclose $50 for two orchestra tickets.
- The price is $7.50 a pound.

3. After shortened forms of proper names, or after contractions of common words, omit the period.

> Joe
> Abe
> memo
> photo
> tech
> math

6:4 APOSTROPHES AND WHERE TO PUT THEM

Apostrophes have three uses:

1. To show possession
2. To indicate omission
3. To indicate the plural of figures, letters, and words mentioned as words

6:4a To Show Possession

This is the most complicated use of the apostrophe, and it causes the most confusion. There are seven rules for this application, the first of which is simplest.

1. Use an *apostrophe* and *s* to form the possessive of a noun not ending in *s.*

> men's
> women's
> secretary's
> executive's

2. Use an *apostrophe alone* to form the possessive of a plural noun ending in *s.*

> secretaries'
> executives'
> employees'

3. Use an *apostrophe* and *s*, or the apostrophe alone, to form the possessive of a singular noun ending in *s.*

the boss's desk
Ms. Jones's [or Jones'] office.

4. Add an *apostrophe* and *s* to the second member of a pair to indicate joint possession.

- We buy our stationery at Benson and Horne's.
- We use Smith and Dunn's office supplies.

5. Add an *apostrophe* and *s* to the last word in a compound.

somebody else's fault
his father-in-law's business

6. The *apostrophe* and *s* are used in the possessive case of indefinite pronouns such as **one, no one, somebody, nobody, someone,** or **another.**

somebody's responsibility
one's day off

7. Never use an apostrophe with the possessive *its* or with **hers, his, yours, theirs, ours,** or **whose.**

Incorrect:	What is **it's** significance?
	Who's turn is it?
Correct:	What is **its** significance?
	Whose turn is it?

6:4b To Indicate Omission

Use an apostrophe to indicate the omission of letters or figures.

won't
doesn't
haven't
July '90

6:4c To Indicate Certain Plurals

An *apostrophe* and *s* indicate the plural of figures, letters, and words in italics or boldface type.

- His 7's look like 4's
- He doesn't dot his *i*'s or cross his *t*'s.
- Our business began in the 1940's.
- Your letter contains too many **and**'s.

Note: It is acceptable to omit the apostrophe when doing so does not cause confusion.

> 1940s
>
> 7s

6:5 THE BASIC USE OF COLONS

As every secretary knows, the basic business use of the colon is after the salutation of a letter.

> Dear Mr. Wayne:
>
> Dear Ms. Johnson:

The next most important use is as an introduction to a list, an explanatory statement, or a long quotation.

- We wish to place our order for the following:
- These are the reasons for our product's popularity:
- The chairperson then stated:

A colon is also used to indicate digital time, to separate chapter and verse from the Bible, or to separate a title from a subtitle.

> 11:30 a.m.
>
> Genesis 45:16
>
> Business Communication: A Guide for the Nineties

6:6 THE LIMITED USE OF DASHES

A secretary may never have the occasion to use a dash in written communication. The use of the dash usually depends on an employer's preference. Dashes can take the place of commas, semicolons, and colons; but their use is preferably limited to marking an abrupt interruption in the thought of a sentence. The dash is formed with two hyphens, and no space should be left between it and the surrounding words.

- It was the packing--not the handling--that was responsible for the breakage.
- The price--I am sure you will agree--is lower than any we have offered so far.
- We have had a number of inquiries--I think there have been a dozen in the past week--concerning our new premium offer.

6:7 PARENTHESES

Parentheses are used to enclose supplementary material that explains or clarifies something else in the sentence. Do not use a comma before a parenthesis.

1. Use parentheses to differentiate between two cities of the same name.

Incorrect:	The Springfield, (MA) General Hospital
Correct:	The Springfield (MA) General Hospital

2. Use parentheses to enclose figures that have been repeated to ensure accuracy.

- We pay two dollars ($2) for typewriter ribbons.
- We have had twenty-five (25) claims for damages.

3. Use a question mark in parentheses to indicate uncertainty.

- I believe the address is 1540(?) Broadway.

4. Use parentheses to enclose the acronym for a title or name when the full title or name is used for the first time.

- The Federal Aviation Administration (FAA) is investigating the cause of the accident.

6:8 HOW TO HANDLE QUOTATION MARKS

Three questions arise in connection with quotation marks:

1. When to use them
2. Where to place punctuation in relation to them
3. Where to place quotation marks in quotes of more than one paragraph

6:8a When to Use Quotes

1. Quotation marks are used when repeating directly and exactly what someone has said.

- The chairperson said, "Our ratings have shown a satisfactory increase."

2. Quotation marks are omitted when repeating words indirectly or inexactly.

- The chairperson said that our ratings have shown an increase.

3. Quotation marks are used to enclose a word or phrase used in a special sense.

- In this instance I'm using "perk" to mean use of the corporate jet.

4. The first time an unusual word or phrase is used, it should be put in quotes, but the quotes are not repeated the second time.

- This group of elderly citizens calls itself "The Gray Panthers." The Gray Panthers fight for equal rights for senior citizens.

5. Quotation marks are used to enclose the titles of articles, short stories, paintings, episodes on television, poems, and songs, unless you type the titles in all caps.

- I read the chapter "Quick and Easy Punctuation" last night.

Note: Quotation marks are sometimes used to enclose the titles of books, periodicals and newspapers, but italics or underlining is generally preferred.

6. Use single quotation marks to enclose a quotation within a quotation.

- The notice reads, "Please endorse your checks, 'Pay to the order of Bankers Trust.' "

Note: Quotation marks always come in pairs. Remember to conclude with them when you have begun that way.

Incorrect:	"I like the progress you have made, he said.
Correct:	"I like the progress you have made," he said.

---

7. A quotation that flows right along with the sentence is not set off by commas.

- They raised their hands to indicate "Yes" or "No."
- The manager said that he would "reduce absenteeism by 20%."

6:8b Where to Place Other Punctuation

1. Commas and periods are placed inside the quotation mark. (See also 6:1g.)

- "I will fly on ahead," she said, "and make all the arrangements for your stay."

2. Colons and semicolons are placed outside quotation marks.

- These items are "hot": roller skates, running shoes, and skis.
- You ordered the shade called "French Taupe"; however, the only shade available is "Tender Tan."

3. Question marks and exclamation marks are placed inside or outside the quotation mark, depending on whether or not they are a part of the quotation.

- She asked us, "Who is responsible for this mistake?"
- Who wrote "Elements of Style"?
- Tell them our answer is, "Absolutely not!"
- Now he tells me, "I cannot attend"!

4. To indicate an omission from a quotation, use three periods in succession.

- He concluded his speech, ". . . and with your help we will succeed."

6:8c Quotes of More Than One Paragraph

When you quote more than one paragraph, put quotation marks at the beginning of each paragraph and at the end of the last paragraph.

Dear Mr. Sweet:

On November 7, I received the following letter from Mr. Lawrence C. Conners of Conners and Doling:

"I have read the copy of the covering letter addressed to you under date of October 30, wherein the Colonial Bank forwarded to you a check in the sum of $1,256.71, representing the final amount due from the Estate of William J. Donovan to the Estate of Harry Donovan.

"I am concerned with this distribution inasmuch as the check is not payable to any legal representative of Jessie Donovan.

"On November 1, I called the Colonial Bank and spoke with Mr. Charles D. Sweet, who is going to look into the matter."

Since I have heard nothing further from Mr. Conners, I would appreciate your bringing me up to date on the status of this case.

Sincerely,

Note: Contemporary business usage allows you to indent long quotes, that is, to move the left and right margins in from the standard margin for paragraphs. With this option, you do not use quotation marks because the narrow text shows the reader what is quoted.

6:9 PUNCTUATION TEST

Here is a sample letter to test you on the punctuation covered in this chapter. Go over it carefully, checking every possible comma, semicolon, colon, apostrophe, period, quotation mark, and parentheses. If you have absorbed the material in this chapter, you should make very few mistakes. The answer follows.

Dear Ms. Williams

By this time you must have received our letter read it and made a decision as to our proposition Mr Robert Graves whom you met when you were here is eager to go ahead

Only this morning Mr Graves asked me have you heard from Ms. Williams and I had to reply No We would appreciate learning your answer it means a great deal to us As Mr Graves assistant I am as eager as he is to see the deal consummated Mr Graves has just taken over his father-in-laws real estate operations and he wants to maintain the firms fine reputation

To repeat our proposal the loft is priced at ninety thousand dollars $90000 and the monthly maintenance charge is $47550 We think its a good offer and we hope to hear from you soon

Sincerely

Answer to Punctuation Test

Dear Ms. Williams:

By this time, you must have received our letter, read it, and made a decision as to our proposition. Mr. Robert Graves, whom you met when you were here, is eager to go ahead.

Only this morning, Mr. Graves asked me, "Have you heard from Ms. Williams?" and I had to reply "No." We would appreciate learning your answer; it means a great deal to us. As Mr. Graves' [or Graves's] assistant, I am as eager as he is to see the deal consummated. Mr. Graves has just taken over his father-in-law's real estate operations, and he wants to maintain the firm's fine reputation.

To repeat our proposal, the loft is priced at ninety thousand dollars ($90,000), and the monthly maintenance charge is $475.50. We think it's a good offer, and we hope to hear from you soon.

Sincerely

7

Helpful Spelling Aids

The three most difficult spelling decisions a secretary must make
are

1. When to drop the final **e** before suffixes like **ing, ly, able,** and **ness.**
2. When to double final consonants before **ing, ed, er,** or **est.**
3. How to spell words using prefixes like **mis, dis,** and **un.**

With the increasingly commonplace use of word processing,
secretaries can rely on spelling checkers for many troublesome
spelling and typographical errors. But even the most sophisticated
software cannot guarantee accuracy. A good grounding in the
basic rules of spelling is still essential.

7.1 SEVEN PRIMARY RULES

The seven rules discussed here should answer most of your questions about spelling. When in doubt, rely on a good dictionary.

7:1a The Silent E

A final silent *e* is usually dropped before a suffix like *able* or *ible*
that begins with a vowel, but it is retained before a suffix like *ness*
or *ly* that begins with a consonant.

advise	advising	advisement
	advisable	

arrive	arrival arriving	
bare	baring	barely, bareness bareback
believe	believing believable	
care	caring	careful, careless carefree
excite	exciting excitable	excitement
extreme	extremist	extremely
hope	hoping	hopeless hopeful
like	likable	likeness likely
live	livable	lively livelihood
love	lovable	lovely lovesick
move	movable	movement
owe	owing	
purchase	purchasing purchasable	
safe		safely, safety safeguard
sincere	sincerity	sincerely
sure		surely surety
use	usable usage	useless useful

Exceptions:

1. The silent *e* is retained when *ing* is added and dropping it would cause confusion with another word, as in *dye* and *dyeing*, which are not to be confused with *die* and *dying*, in which the final *e* in *die* has been changed to *y*.

2. The silent *e* is retained before a suffix beginning with a vowel in order to simplify pronunciation, as in *acre, acreage; here, herein; mile, mileage; there, therein.*

3. The silent *e* is dropped before a suffix beginning with a consonant in certain common words like *abridgment, acknowl-*

edgment, argument, awful, doubly, duly, incredibly, judgment, possibly, probably, truly, wholly.

    Note: Some words like *judgment* and **acknowledgment** now have an acceptable alternate spelling of *judgement* and **acknowledgement**, probably because so many people spell them this way all the time. Purists prefer to eliminate the silent *e*.

    4. The silent *e* is retained in words ending with **ce** or **ge** to keep the soft sound of the *c* or *g*, even when the suffix begins with a vowel, as in **advantageous, changeable, outrageous, noticeable,** and **serviceable**.

7:1b   Double or Not

The rule for doubling final consonants can be divided into two parts.

    1. Words of one syllable that end in a single consonant preceded by a single vowel double the consonant when followed by a suffix beginning with a vowel.

> clan, clannish
> drop, dropped, dropping
> shop, shopper, shopped, shopping
> plan, planned, planning, planner
> red, redder, reddest, redden, reddish
> run, running, runner

Exception: The letter *x* is never doubled.
> fix, fixing, fixable, fixation
> tax, taxes, taxing, taxable, taxation

    2. Words of more than one syllable, accented on the last syllable and ending in a single consonant preceded by a single vowel, double the consonant when followed by a suffix beginning with a vowel.

> acquit, acquitted, acquitting, acquittal
> admit, admitted, admitting, admittance
> begin, beginner, beginning
> control, controlled, controller, controlling, controllable

> equip, equipped, equipping
> forget, forgetting, forgettable, unforgettable
> occur, occurred, occurring, occurrence
> overlap, overlapped, overlapping
> prefer, preferred, preferring
> refer, referred, referring, referral
> transfer, transferred, transferring

Exceptions:

1. Words in which the accent changes to another syllable when the suffix is added, do not double the final consonant.

> confer, conference
> defer, deference
> infer, inference
> prefer, preference, preferable

2. Words ending in a final consonant preceded by two vowels do not double the final consonant.

> appear, appeared, appearing, appearance
> reveal, revealed, revealing

3. Words ending in two consonants do not double the final consonant.

> insist, insisted, insistence, insistent
> invent, invented, inventor

4. Words not accented on the final syllable usually do not double the final consonant.

> credit, credited, creditor
> happen, happened, happening
> moisten, moistened, moistening

7:1c MIS, DIS, and UN

Words beginning with *mis* or *dis* offer so many opportunities for mistakes that they can baffle the most expert secretary. Take, for example, *disappoint*. It often is spelled *dissappoint, disapoint,* or *dissapoint. Misspell* is another such word. Is it *mispell, misspel,* or *misppell*?

A good rule to remember is that only about 40 common words begin with *diss* or *miss*, while closer to 400 words begin with *dis* or *mis*.

You will make fewer errors if you separate the prefix from the root word. Thus, in *disappoint*, the root word is *appoint*, so only one *s* is required. In *misspell* the root word is *spell*, so naturally there must be two *s*'s.

The prefix *un* follows the same formula. When the root word begins with *n*, there will be two *n*'s; when the root word begins with another letter, there will be one *n*.

> unnatural, unnecessary, unnegotiable, unnoticed
> unabridged, unavoidable, unconditional, unlimited

7:1d ABLE and IBLE

The primary rule for the *able/ible* quandary is that the ending should be *able* if the base is a complete word and *ible* if the base is not a complete word.

acceptable	audible
available	collapsible
breakable	combustible
comfortable	compatible
commendable	credible
considerable	divisible
dependable	edible
detectable	eligible
discreditable	feasible
drinkable	forcible
fashionable	incorrigible
favorable	indelible
noticeable	infallible
perishable	intelligible
predictable	irresistible
presentable	negligible
profitable	ostensible
readable	plausible
taxable	tangible
workable	visible

ABLE Exceptions:

1. The ending is *able* if the base word has dropped the final *e*, such as *believable, debatable, desirable, excitable, excusable, likable, presumable, sizable,* and *valuable.*

2. The ending is *able* if the base word ended in a *y* which has been changed to *i*, such as *classifiable, enviable, justifiable,* and *reliable.*

3. The ending is usually *able* if the base ends in a hard *c* or a hard *g*, like the sound of *c* in *cut* or the *g* in *got*. Examples include *amicable, applicable, explicable, implacable, navigable, practicable,* and *irrevocable.*

In the case of *able*, there are exceptions to the exceptions, and you will have to try to memorize words such as *equitable, inevitable, memorable, palpable,* and *vulnerable,* which follow no rule.

IBLE Exceptions:

1. The ending should usually be *ible* if the base can form another word with the addition of *ion* or *sion*. For example, *perfect/perfection/perfectible*. Other such words are *accessible, collectible, connectible, convertible, corruptible, digestible, reversible, suggestible*. Some words, like *detect*, are exceptions to the exception: *detect/detection/detectable.*

2. Some bases ending in *ss* have *ible* endings, even though they are complete words in themselves: *dismissible, accessible,* and *remissible.*

3. The ending is usually *ible* if the base ends in a soft *c* like *reduce*, or a soft *g* like *intelligent*. Examples include *eligible, forcible, illegible, intangible, intelligible, invincible, legible, negligible, producible,* and *reducible.*

In the case of *ible*, there are some words that follow no particular rule and which you can only try to memorize, such as *collapsible, contemptible, discernible, flexible, gullible,* and *resistible.*

7:1e LY, LLY, and ALLY

When forming an adverb from an adjective, the suffix *ly* is added to the word, as in *rich/richly*, or *cruel/cruelly*. If the word already ends in *al*, the ending will be *ally*, as in *actual/actually*.

If the adjective ends in *ic*, the adverb also ends in **ally**, as in **automatically**, **basically**, **emphatically**, **grammatically**, and **systematically**. The only exception to this rule is the word **publicly**.

7:1f ANCE and ENCE

If the verb ends in an *r* preceded by a vowel and is accented on the last syllable, the noun is formed with **ence: coherence, conference, deference, inference, preference, reference**.

Otherwise, there is no uniform rule for **ance** and **ence** endings.

7:1g IE and EI

If you remember only one spelling rule from grade school, it's probably the following:

- *I* before *e*, except after *c*, or when sounded like *a*, as in **neighbor** and **weigh**.

Words like **believe** and **receive** sound alike but are spelled differently. You can trust the rule for most cases.

Exceptions: Some words are spelled with *ei* combinations even though they don't follow the rule. These include **either, neither, foreign, height, leisure, weird, seizure**, and **sheik**.

7:2 100 COMMONLY MISSPELLED WORDS

Choose the correct spelling for each word.

	A	B
1.	absence	abcense
2.	acommodate	accommodate
3.	achievement	achievment
4.	acquiesce	aquiesce
5.	alloted	allotted
6.	analyse	analyze
7.	approximate	aproximate
8.	argument	arguement
9.	assistent	assistant
10.	attendance	attendence

11. banana	bananna
12. begining	beginning
13. believe	beleive
14. changeable	changable
15. collosal	colossal
16. commitment	comitment
17. commitee	committee
18. consede	concede
19. conscientious	consientious
20. consensus	concensus
21. controversy	contreversy
22. criticise	criticize
23. desperate	desparate
24. develope	develop
25. dictionery	dictionary
26. dissapoint	disappoint
27. discriminate	discrimminate
28. drastically	drasticly
29. efficiancy	efficiency
30. eligable	eligible
31. embarrass	embarass
32. exagerate	exaggerate
33. existence	existance
34. forty	fourty
35. friend	freind
36. fullfil	fulfill
37. grammar	grammer
38. imediately	immediately
39. inadvertant	inadvertent
40. infallible	infallable
41. insistent	insistant
42. intersede	intercede
43. interestting	interesting
44. interfered	interferred
45. knowlege	knowledge
46. lisence	license
47. liquefy	liquify
48. loneliness	lonelyness
49. maintanence	maintenance

50.	managment	management
51.	millionaire	millionnaire
52.	morgaged	mortgaged
53.	nickle	nickel
54.	niece	neice
55.	ninty-ninth	ninety-ninth
56.	occasionally	ocasionally
57.	occurrence	occurence
58.	paralyze	paralize
59.	permissable	permissible
60.	persistant	persistent
61.	persuade	pursuade
62.	Polaroid	Poleroid
63.	preceding	preceeding
64.	predictible	predictable
65.	preferable	preferible
66.	presumptuous	presumtuous
67.	privelige	privilege
68.	psycological	psychological
69.	publicly	publically
70.	pursuit	persuit
71.	questionaire	questionnaire
72.	quizzes	quizes
73.	receive	recieve
74.	recipiant	recipient
75.	reccomend	recommend
76.	refered	referred
77.	repell	repel
78.	repitition	repetition
79.	rhythm	rythm
80.	safety	safty
81.	sieze	seize
82.	sincerly	sincerely
83.	sincerety	sincerity
84.	skillful	skilfull
85.	souvenir	souvenier
86.	specemin	specimen
87.	sueing	suing
88.	superintendant	superintendent

89. supercede	supersede
90. suprise	surprise
91. their	thier
92. transferable	transferible
93. truly	truely
94. unparalleled	unparalelled
95. usage	useage
96. vegetible	vegetable
97. vitious	vicious
98. Wednesday	Wednsday
99. weird	wierd
100. writeing	writing

Answers to the spelling quiz are at the end of this chapter.

Tips for Correct Answers

1. The seven primary spelling rules should have helped you determine the correct spelling of many of the preceding words: words ending in *ible, able*; words ending in *ing, ness,* or *ly*; words beginning with *mis, dis,* or *un*; words with *ie* or *ei*.

2. *ery* and *ary*: Only six common words end in *ery*: *cemetery, confectionery, distillery, millinery, monastery,* and *stationery* (meaning writing materials). All the rest end in *ary*, such as *secretary*.

3. *ise, ize, yze*: Only two common words end in *yze*: *analyze* and *paralyze*. The majority of the rest end in *ize*, like *authorize, modernize,* or *specialize*. The balance end in *ise*, and you will have to try to remember them. They are the *cise* words, like *exercise*; the *guise* words, like *disguise*; the *mise* words, like *compromise*; the *rise* words, like *sunrise*; the *vise* words, like *advise*; the *wise* words, like *likewise*; and various others, like *advertise* or *merchandise*.

4. *cede, ceed, sede*: Only one word in English ends in *sede*, and that is *supersede*. Only three words end in *ceed*; they are *exceed, proceed,* and *succeed*. The remaining words with this ending are spelled with *cede*, such as *recede*.

5. *efy* and *ify*: A few words, like *stupefy* and *liquefy*, use the *efy* ending. All the rest are spelled with *ify*.

7:3 CAPITALIZATION GUIDELINES

The first word of every sentence should be capitalized, as well as the names of people, countries, cities, and streets.

> Mr. Andrew Barber
> 215 Downing Street
> London, England

This rule is generally well known. Other rules for capitalization may be less well known.

7:3a Quotations

Capitalize the first word of every direct quotation.

- She said, "Business is improving in all of our branches."

Do not capitalize the first word in an indirect quotation.

- She said that business was improving.

7:3b Titles

Titles are capitalized when they refer to specific persons.

the President	Mother
Senator Johnson	Father

Do not capitalize titles if they are used in a general sense, referring to a class of persons.

- A president has certain specific duties.
- Two senators are elected from each state.

Do not capitalize the names of relatives if they are preceded by possessives.

- My mother is out of town.
- My brother looks very much as Father did at his age.

7:3c Deity and Religions

Capitalize names for the Deity, including personal pronouns. Capitalize names for the Bible and other sacred writings, and the names of religions and religious groups.

- God, Jesus Christ, He, Him
- Bible, Koran, Torah, the Scriptures, Book of Genesis
- Protestant, Catholic, Jewish, Shinto, Buddhist

7:3d Days and Months

Days and months are capitalized, but the seasons are not.

- Wednesday, Thursday, Friday
- June, July, August
- spring, summer, autumn

7:3e Schools and Universities

Names of schools and universities are capitalized, but only when referring to a particular institution.

- Harvard University
- Barnard College
- Evander Childs High School
- She is a high school graduate.
- She attended college in California.

7:3f Sections of the Country

Capitalize particular sections of the country, but do not capitalize the points of the compass.

- she lives in the South.
- She drove north to New York City.

7:3g Races and Organizations

Capitalize the names of races and organizations.

- Indian, Caucasian, Occidental, and Oriental

- League of Women Voters
- National Organization for Women
- National Secretaries Association

7:3h Books, Plays, and Magazines

All important words, including the first word, in the titles of books, plays, and magazines should be capitalized.

- *The Last of the Mohicans*
- *Who's Afraid of Virginia Woolf?*
- *The New Yorker*

Note: When typing, underline the titles of books, plays, and magazines. When using a word processor with italic type, italic is preferred.

Answers to Spelling Test

1. A	21. A	41. A	61. A	81. B
2. B	22. B	42. B	62. A	82. B
3. A	23. A	43. B	63. A	83. B
4. A	24. B	44. A	64. B	84. A
5. B	25. B	45. B	65. A	85. A
6. B	26. B	46. B	66. A	86. B
7. A	27. A	47. A	67. B	87. B
8. A	28. A	48. A	68. B	88. B
9. B	29. B	49. B	69. A	89. B
10. A	30. B	50. B	70. A	90. B
11. A	31. A	51. A	71. B	91. A
12. B	32. B	52. B	72. A	92. A
13. A	33. A	53. B	73. A	93. A
14. A	34. A	54. A	74. B	94. A
15. B	35. A	55. B	75. B	95. A
16. A	36. B	56. A	76. B	96. B
17. B	37. A	57. A	77. B	97. B
18. B	38. B	58. A	78. B	98. A
19. A	39. B	59. B	79. A	99. A
20. A	40. A	60. B	80. A	100. B

8

Word Division

In the past, secretaries frequently had to decide when to divide a word when they typed letters and memos. If a word at the end of a line would stick out too far into the right margin, it had to be divided, or hyphenated. The secretary had to know the rules of word division or look up each word in a dictionary or spell check reference. Fortunately, with word processing becoming so common in the modern office, secretaries can forget about dividing or hyphenating because the software "wraps" words that are too long down to the next line.

Many software packages feature a hyphenation command that allows a word that breaks at the end of a line to be hyphenated in the correct place automatically, since the software relies on its dictionary to know where to break the word. In sophisticated packages, the secretary can select "soft hyphens" for word divisions that will disappear if text is added or deleted, causing the length of the line to change. In other instances, compound words that must be hyphenated will remain together with a "hard hyphen" selection, even when the line of text changes.

This chapter covers the rules for dividing words and for forming compound words with hyphens. Until everyone has computers capable of doing these tasks automatically, it's a good idea to know the rules.

8:1   TEN CONCISE RULES

1. Words of more than two syllables are divided on a vowel, unless such division interferes with correct pronunciation.

abdi-cate	centi-grade
geno-cide	para-noid

But **not**: gala-xy or homo-genize

2. Separate double consonants, unless it means breaking up a root word.

ban-ning	dun-ning
reces-sion	win-ner

But **not**: fil-ling or instal-ling

3. Separate two consonants preceded and followed by vowels.

domes-tic
mis-sile
ren-dered

4. To avoid confusion, hyphenated compounds should be divided at the hyphen, and nonhyphenated compounds should be divided between the two basic words.

Hyphenated	Nonhyphenated
Latin-American	back-ground
self-addressed	age-less
above-mentioned	air-wave
half-truth	stock-holder

5. Do not divide contractions.

hasn't
wouldn't

6. Do not separate the first letter of a word from the rest.

adept
eclipse
icicle
opaque

7. Do not divide a four-letter word, and only rarely divide a five-letter word.

> decoy
> defy
> lucky
> many
> pity
> idle

8. Do not divide words that are pronounced as one syllable, no matter how many letters are involved.

> drought
> friend
> wrought
> schism

9. Avoid the separation of two-letter syllables at the beginnings of words with three or more syllables.

aspi-rin	**not**	as-pirin
inten-tion	**not**	in-tention
unfor-tunate	**not**	un-fortunate

10. Do not divide words at the ends of two successive lines or the last word in a paragraph.

8:2 PROPER NOUNS

Do not divide proper nouns if it can be avoided, especially the names of persons, and do not separate the initials from the rest of the name.

When division of proper nouns cannot be avoided, follow the general rules of hyphenation.

Abra-ham	Cleo-patra
Man-hattan	Lon-don
B. Alt-man	Rome
Adolph	Leo-pold

8:3 PREFIXES

A prefix is a syllable that is put before a word and changes its meaning. Such a word is usually divided on the prefix, although it is preferable not to separate a two-letter prefix.

8:3a Three-Letter Prefix

Words with three-letter prefixes can usually be divided conveniently on the prefix.

> dis-color
> pre-dominant
> pro-cession

8:3b Two-Syllable Prefix

Prefixes of more than one syllable are usually preserved intact to make the meaning clear.

> ante
> anti
> hyper
> inter
> macro
> micro
> multi
> over
> poly
> retro
> semi
> ultra

8:3c Two-Letter Prefix

Although it should be avoided whenever possible, words with two-letter prefixes can be divided on the prefix when absolutely necessary.

> ab-sent
> ad-verb
> de-cline
> de-scribe

in-duce
ob-ject
re-store
un-happy

8:4   SUFFIXES

Suffixes are added to the ends of base words to modify the meaning or change the usage.

8:4a   Avoiding Two-Letter Carryovers

Carrying over two-letter endings should be avoided, especially in words of more than three syllables.

instabil-ity	**not**	instabili-ty
adver-tiser	**not**	advertis-er
vegetar-ian	**not**	vegetari-an

Exception: A sounded *ed* ending can be carried over.

inflat-ed   but **never**   propos-ed

8:4b   Division of Two-Letter Carryovers

Sometimes two-letter carryovers cannot be avoided because the root word would be improperly broken up.

announc-er	**not**	announ-cer
examin-er	**not**	exami-ner
observ-er	**not**	obser-ver

Exception: Words ending in *or*, with a preceding consonant, are usually divided before the consonant.

administra-tor
counse-lor
supervi-sor

8:4c   IBLE and ABLE

The suffixes *able* and *ible* are usually carried over.

compat-ible	collaps-ible
predict-able	fashion-able

Exceptions:

inflam-mable
memo-rable
irrespon-sible

8:4d Positively Indivisible Suffixes

Some suffixes cannot be broken up under any circumstances.
Some examples follow.

commer-cial	ini-tial	controver-sial
suspi-cion	ten-sion	igni-tion
gra-cious	preten-tious	herba-ceous
gor-geous	reli-gious	re-gion

8:4e The ING Suffix

Words ending in ***ing*** are divided on the base word, unless the final
consonant is doubled.

enlist-ing	report-ing	review-ing
omit-ting	infer-ring	get-ting

Exception: When the word ends in a silent vowel preceded by
two consonants, the final consonant or consonants become part of
the suffix.

trou-bling
bun-dling
med-dling
trick-ling

8:4f The METER Suffix

When ***meter*** is pronounced with a long *e* as in ***kilometer***, the suffix
meter should not be divided.

kilo-meter
centi-meter
milli-meter

Exception: When it is pronounced with a short *e*, as in the
word ***speedometer***, the division comes after the ***m***.

speedom-eter
barom-eter
thermom-eter

8:5 WORD DIVISION TEST

1. Which of the following divisions of the word *duplicate* is correct?

   a. du-plicate
   b. duplic-ate
   c. dupli-cate

2. How would you divide *centered*?

3. Where would you divide *centerpiece*?

4. Which of the following are correct?

   a. ham-mer
   b. progress-ive
   c. install-ing
   d. proces-sing

5. How would you divide the following?

   a. doesn't
   b. haven't
   c. thought
   d. frowned
   e. only

6. What is the correct division of these words?

   a. antidote
   b. discussion
   c. overcome
   d. debated

7. Where would you divide these suffixes?

   a. disciplinarian
   b. adviser
   c. guarantor

8. Pick out the wrong division(s) among the following:

   a. comfort-able
   b. formid-able
   c. dura-ble
   d. manage-able

9. Pick out the wrong division(s) among the following:

    a. expan-sion
    b. recogni-tion
    c. essen-tial
    d. provinc-ial
    e. deli-cious

10. What is wrong with the word divisions in this paragraph?

Although we cannot extend credit privileges
at the present time, we would be happy to ship merchandise to you on C.O.D. terms. Perhaps in the future, if you try us again, we may be able to reconsider.

The answers to this test are at the end of this chapter.

8:6 TWO-SYLLABLE WORD DIVISION LIST

Words of two syllables are split at the end of the first syllable, as
indicated in this list.

A	ar-row	bill-board	can-did
ab-duct	art-ist	blan-ket	can-dor
ab-rupt	as-pect	bla-tant	can-not
ab-sent	as-tute	blink-er	can-vass
ac-cent	at-las	block-ade	ca-reer
ac-tor	at-tain	bod-ice	cash-ier
ad-age		bond-age	ca-ter
ad-mire	**B**	bo-nus	cen-sor
af-firm	bab-ble	bor-der	cen-sus
af-ter	bag-gy	bro-ken	cer-tain
ag-ile	bal-ance	bur-den	chal-lenge
al-bum	ban-ish	bu-reau	chap-ter
al-ter	bank-er	bur-glar	cher-ish
am-bush	bap-tise		cho-rus
an-chor	bar-ber	**C**	Christ-mas
an-ger	ba-sis	ca-ble	cir-cuit
an-nul	beau-ty	caf-feine	clas-sic
ap-peal	be-gin	cal-lous	cleav-age
ar-rest	be-nign	cam-pus	cli-max
ar-rive	be-quest	can-cel	col-late

D

dai-ly
dam-age
Dan-ish
dar-ing
de-bate
debt-or
dec-ade
de-fer
de-gree
del-uge
den-tal
de-rive
des-pot
de-tain
de-tect
dic-tate
dif-fer
di-rect
dis-bar
dis-burse
dis-cuss
di-vide
dol-lar
doz-en
driv-en

E

ear-nest
ea-sel
ef-fect
ef-fort
eight-een
ei-ther
el-bow
em-bark
em-blem
em-pire

em-ploy
en-chant
en-close
en-dorse
en-roll
ep-och
er-mine
er-rand
er-ror
es-cape
es-say
es-trange
eth-ics
eth-nic
ex-act

F

fab-ric
fac-et
fac-tion
fac-tor
fail-ure
far-ther
fash-ion
fa-tigue
fa-vor
fea-ture
feed-back
fel-low
fe-male
fer-tile
fes-tive
fi-ber
fic-tion
fig-ure
fil-ter
fix-ture
fla-grant

flip-pant
flour-ish
flu-ent
frac-tion

G

gal-ley
gal-lon
ga-lore
gam-ble
gar-nish
gas-tric
gen-der
ge-nial
gen-ius
gent-ly
ges-ture
gi-ant
glar-ing
glob-al
glos-sy
gold-en
gor-geous
gos-pel
gos-sip
gour-met
grate-ful
grim-ace
gro-tesque
grue-some
gus-to

H

hab-it
hal-ter
ham-per
hand-some

har-ass
har-ness
haz-ard
health-ful
heav-en
hel-met
hence-forth
her-mit
her-self
hey-day
hid-den
hin-drance
hob-by
hock-ey
hold-er
hol-low
hon-or
hook-up
hos-tage
hu-man
hus-band

I

ig-nite
ig-nore
im-age
im-bibe
im-mense
im-pede
im-ply
in-ane
in-born
in-cline
in-dex
in-fringe
in-vite
irk-some
is-land

is-sue
it-self

J

jack-et
jar-gon
jew-el
jock-ey
jos-tle
jour-ney
joy-ful
jum-bo
jus-tice

K

ka-pok
ken-nel
ker-nel
kid-nap
kind-ly
knowl-edge
knuck-le
ku-dos

L

la-bor
lac-quer
la-ment
lam-poon
lan-guage
lan-tern
large-ly
lar-ynx
la-tent
laun-der
lav-ish
leak-age
leath-er

lec-ture
ledg-er
le-gal
leg-end
lei-sure
le-thal
li-cense
lim-it
lin-guist
liq-uid
lis-ten
lo-cal
log-ic
look-out
lum-ber
lunch-eon
lus-cious
lyr-ic

M

ma-chine
mag-ic
mag-net
main-tain
ma-jor
mal-ice
ma-lign
mam-moth
man-age
man-ner
mar-gin
mar-ket
mar-riage
mas-cot
mas-sage
match-less
ma-tron
mat-ter

ma-ture
meas-ure
med-al
mem-oir
men-tion
mer-cy
mes-sage
mi-grate
mil-lion
mi-nor
mo-lest
mon-ey
mor-al
mor-bid
muf-fle

N

na-ive
nap-kin
nar-rate
na-tive
na-ture
neck-lace
nee-dle
ne-glect
nei-ther
neph-ew
neu-tral
nick-el
non-sense
nor-mal
note-book
no-tice
no-tion
nour-ish
nov-ice
nui-sance
num-ber

nup-tial
nur-ture
nut-shell
ny-lon

O

oat-meal
ob-ject
ob-long
ob-scene
ob-scure
oc-cult
oc-cur
oc-tave
of-fend
of-fer
of-fice
of-ten
on-set
op-pose
op-press
op-tion
or-ange
or-bit
or-der
or-nate
or-phan
os-trich
oth-er
own-er

P

pack-age
pad-lock
pag-eant
pal-ace
pal-ate
pal-lid

pam-per
pam-phlet
pan-der
pan-el
pan-ic
pa-per
pa-rade
par-cel
par-don
par-ent
par-lor
part-ner
pas-sage
pat-ent
pa-tron
pe-nal
pen-ance
pen-sion
peo-ple
per-ceive
per-form
per-son
pho-to
pick-et
pic-nic
pic-ture
pin-point
pi-rate
pit-fall
pla-cate
plain-tiff
plas-tic
pleas-ant
plu-ral
po-lite
pol-lute
por-trait
pos-sess
pos-ture

pre-cede
pri-vate
pro-claim
pur-pose

Q

quag-mire
Quak-er
quar-rel
quar-ter
que-ry
quib-ble
qui-et
quin-tet
quo-rum

R

rab-bit
ra-cial
ra-cism
ra-dar
ran-cor
rau-cous
re-act
rea-son
re-bate
re-cap
re-ceipt
re-cent
re-cord (v.)
rec-ord (n.)
re-deem
ref-uge
re-gret
re-ject
ren-der
re-new
rent-al

re-pair
re-place
re-ply
re-port
rep-tile
re-quest
re-serve
res-pite
re-sponse
re-tail
re-vise
rig-id
ros-trum
ro-tate
ruf-fle
rup-ture
ruth-less

S

sa-cred
safe-ty
sa-lute
sanc-tion
sat-ire
sav-age
scan-dal
schol-ar
sci-ence
scrip-ture
sea-son
se-cret
seg-ment
se-quel
se-ries
shel-ter
short-age
sig-nal
sim-ple

slan-der
so-ber
som-ber
sor-ry
spe-cial
squan-der
squeam-ish
stand-ard
stat-ute
sten-cil
strin-gent
struc-ture
sub-ject
sub-mit
sub-stance
sub-tle
sum-mon
su-preme
symp-tom

T

tab-loid
tac-it
tac-tics
tal-ent
tam-per
tar-get
tem-per
ten-ant
ten-sion
tex-ture
ther-mal
the-sis
thou-sand
through-out
ti-rade
ti-tle
top-ic

to-tal	up-ward	vi-sion	wom-an
trac-tion	ur-gent		won-der
tran-scend	ut-most	**W**	wor-ry
tran-scribe			writ-ten
trans-fer		wa-ger	
trans-pose	**V**	wait-ress	
trau-ma		wak-en	
trus-tee	va-cant	warn-ing	**Y**
typ-ist	val-id	waste-ful	
	van-ish	wel-come	yearn-ing
	ven-ture	wheth-er	yon-der
	ver-bose	wid-ow	youth-ful
U	ver-sus	will-ful	
	vi-brate	wis-dom	**Z**
ul-cer	vic-tim	wish-ful	
un-der	vir-tue	wit-ness	zeal-ous
un-less			ze-nith
			zip-per

8:7   THREE-SYLLABLE WORD DIVISION LIST

Words of three syllables are ordinarily divided on the vowel, but there are many other factors involved. If you stop to pronounce the word, the division will usually be obvious.

Vowel:	fugi-tive	barri-cade	cere-al
Other:	aban-don	deben-ture	effec-tive

A	addi-tion	ambi-tion	bicy-cle
	ade-quate	anno-tate	bind-ery
abdi-cate	adjec-tive	appar-ent	biweek-ly
abdo-men	admis-sion	appre-hend	blandish-ment
abey-ance	advan-tage	aque-duct	body-guard
abnor-mal	adver-tise	arbi-trate	book-keeper
abol-ish	advo-cate	ascer-tain	broad-cast
abro-gate	affec-tion	atten-tion	broker-age
acci-dent	agen-da	audi-ence	bulle-tin
accli-mate	aggra-vate	aver-age	busi-ness
accom-plish	aggre-gate		
accred-it	alco-hol	**B**	
accu-rate	alli-ance		**C**
accus-tom	alma-nac	bache-lor	
acknowl-edge	alter-nate	bank-ruptcy	Cadil-lac
actu-al		bear-able	calcu-late

calen-dar
cam-era
capa-cious
capi-tal
carni-val
casi-no
cata-lyst
celi-bate
cen-tury
cer-tify
chan-cellor
chap-eron
char-acter
charis-ma
chloro-form
chro-mium
circu-lar
circum-stance
clas-sify
cogni-zant
colos-sal
commer-cial
compan-ion
com-pensate
compe-tence
compli-cate
compro-mise
concen-trate
conde-scend
condi-tion
conse-quence
con-sider
consum-mate
contem-plate
contra-dict
conver-sion
corpo-rate
coura-geous
cred-ible
cubi-cle

cur-sory
cus-tomer
cylin-der

D

deben-ture
decep-tion
deci-sive
deco-rum
dedi-cate
defi-cit
dehy-drate
delin-quent
demar-cate
depos-it
depre-cate
depres-sion
desig-nate
deter-gent
devi-ate
diag-nose
dia-gram
differ-ence
diffi-cult
disci-pline
dispos-sess
diver-sion
docu-ment
dupli-cate

E

eccen-tric
edu-cate
effi-cient
elec-tric
elo-quence
embez-zle
emi-nence
empha-sis
encom-pass

engen-der
enor-mous
epi-gram
eru-dite
estab-lish
eti-quette
euphe-mism
evi-dence
exam-ine
excur-sion
exe-cute
exer-cise
ex-hibit
expe-dite
explo-sion
extra-dite

F

fabri-cate
face-tious
feasi-ble
femi-nine
fero-cious
ficti-tious
flabber-gast
flex-ible
fluctu-ate
for-ever
formal-ize
formu-late
forti-tude
frater-nal
frivo-lous
frustra-tion
furni-ture
fuse-lage

G

gal-axy
galva-nize

garru-lous
gen-eral
genu-ine
gigan-tic
glos-sary
govern-ment
gradu-ate
grati-tude
guaran-tee
gyro-scope

H

handi-cap
haphaz-ard
hemi-sphere
hesi-tate
holi-ness
homi-cide
hori-zon
hospi-tal
how-ever
hurri-cane
hydrau-lic
hydro-gen
hypno-sis

I

idi-om
ille-gal
illu-sive
imag-ine
imma-ture
immi-grate
impair-ment
impar-tial
impend-ing
impe-tus
imple-ment
impos-tor
impro-vise

incen-tive
inci-dent
incom-plete
incor-rect
incum-bent
indi-cate
indus-try
iner-tia
infil-trate
influ-ence
ingen-ious
inhu-man
injus-tice
inno-vate
insin-cere
insti-tute
insu-late
irri-tate
iso-late

J

jani-tor
jeop-ardy
judi-cial
juve-nile

K

kine-scope
know-ingly

L

laby-rinth
lami-nate
lassi-tude
lati-tude
legi-ble
legis-late
lever-age

licen-tious
limit-less
liqui-date
liter-ate
litho-graph
longi-tude
loqua-cious
lubri-cate
lucra-tive

M

macro-cosm
maga-zine
malcon-tent
mali-cious
maneu-ver
mani-fest
mara-thon
mascu-line
matri-arch
maxi-mum
medi-ate
mesmer-ize
meta-phor
micro-phone
mini-mum
miscon-strue
moder-ate
modi-cum
modu-late
momen-tous
mono-logue
moti-vate
multi-ply
muti-late

N

natu-ral
navi-gate

nebu-lous
negli-gent
neuro-sis
nico-tine
nitro-gen
noctur-nal
nomi-nal
noncha-lant
nota-tion
Novem-ber
numer-ous
nutri-ent

O

obli-gate
obnox-ious
obso-lete
occa-sion
occu-pant
odi-ous
offi-cial
oper-ate
opin-ion
oppor-tune
opti-mum
ordi-nance
orna-ment
ostra-cize
ova-tion
over-draft
owner-ship

P

pala-tial
pali-sade
palpi-tate
panto-mime
para-digm

paral-lel
para-phrase
parti-san
pater-nal
patri-cian
pecul-iar
pedes-tal
pene-trate
percep-tive
perfo-rate
perma-nent
permis-sion
perpe-trate
pessi-mist
photo-graph
physi-cal
pictur-esque
pinna-cle
piti-less
plati-tude
plausi-ble
plebe-ian
polar-ize
popu-lar
poten-tial
practi-cal
preco-cious
preju-dice
prema-ture
presi-dent
previ-ous
procre-ate
prodi-gious
profes-sion
propi-tious
prose-cute
provi-sion
psycho-sis
publi-cize

Q

quadru-ped
quadru-ple
quaran-tine
queru-lous
quintes-sence

R

racon-teur
radi-ant
read-able
reaf-firm
real-ize
rebut-tal
recep-tion
recog-nize
recon-cile
redun-dant
refresh-ment
regi-ment
regis-ter
regu-late
rela-tive
reli-ant
remem-ber
reno-vate
reper-toire
repos-sess
repre-sent
repro-duce
requi-site
respon-sive
retro-spect

reve-nue
ridi-cule
rudi-ment
ruin-ous
rumi-nate

S

sacra-ment
sacri-fice
sacro-sanct
satel-lite
sati-ate
satu-rate
scholas-tic
scintil-late
seces-sion
secu-lar
seda-tion
segre-gate
seman-tics
sensa-tion
sepa-rate
sever-ance
signa-ture
simi-lar
sine-cure
singu-lar
skele-ton
soli-taire
solu-tion
sopho-more
souve-nir
speci-men
specu-late

statis-tics
stimu-late
strenu-ous
stupen-dous
subcon-scious
subli-mate
submis-sion
subse-quent
substand-ard
subter-fuge
suffi-cient
sum-mary
supe-rior
super-sede
surro-gate
surveil-lance

T

tabu-late
tangi-ble
tanta-mount
tedi-ous
tele-cast
tele-type
tena-cious
tenta-tive
termi-nate
thermo-stat
titil-late
toler-ant
topi-cal
tourna-ment
tracta-ble
trans-action

trans-fusion
trans-parent
treas-urer
trium-phant
turbu-lent

U

ulti-mate
uncom-mon
under-neath
unfaith-ful
unfas-ten
union-ize
uni-verse
unti-tled
uti-lize

V

vaca-tion
vacil-late
vari-ous
vindi-cate
voca-tion
vola-tile
volun-teer

W

who-ever
wilder-ness
with-drawal
wonder-ful
workman-
  ship

8:8   TO HYPHENATE OR NOT

Compound nouns go through a certain progression as they become more commonly used. At first they appear as two words, then as a hyphenated word, and finally as just one word. Some examples of this are the following:

book case	book-case	bookcase
half back	half-back	halfback
rail road	rail-road	railroad

When in doubt about a compound word, consult your dictionary.

8:8a Compound Adjectives

Hyphenate an adjective consisting of two or more words when it is followed by a noun.

- She is a good-natured person.
- She is good natured.
- This is the best-known book on the subject.
- This book is the best known.

8:8b Suspension Hyphens

When a noun is separated from several modifiers that require the use of a hyphen, the suspension hyphen is used.

- The current rates for first-, second-, and third-class travel are enclosed.
- The new program will have both short- and long-range effects.

8:8c Numbers and Fractions

Compound numerals from *twenty-one* through *ninety-nine* use the hyphen. So do fractions like *one-half* when they function as modifiers.

sixty-seven
one hundred and thirty-eight
three and three-quarters
one-eighth inch

8:8d   Three- and Four-Part Compounds

Three- and four-part compounds use the hyphen in most circumstances.

free-for-all	jack-in-the-box
four-in-hand	jack-of-all-trades
hit-and-run (u.m.)*	run-of-the-mill (u.m.)*
son-in-law	mother-in-law

*u.m. means that the expression is hyphenated only when used as a unit modifier, as in a **hit-and-run** driver.

8:8e   Do Not Hyphenate

1. Do not hyphenate a combination of adverb and adjective when the adverb ends in *ly*.

- He was a highly qualified candidate.
- It is freshly cooked food.

2. Do not hyphenate a fraction that is used as a noun and followed by *of*.

- The paragraph runs for three quarters of a page.

3. Do not use a hyphen between double terms that denote a single office or rank.

> Vice President Smith
> Rear Admiral Jones

4. Prefixes *inter*, *non*, *semi*, and *sub* do not take hyphens unless they are used with proper nouns.

> interchange
> nonprofit
> semiautomatic
> substandard
> non-Caucasian
> non-Christian

Answers to Word Division Test

1. c
2. cen-tered
3. center-piece
4. a and c
5. Do not divide any.
6. anti-dote   over-come
   discus-sion   debat-ed
7. disciplinar-ian, advis-er, guaran-tor
8. b. It should be **formidable** or **formida-ble**.
9. d. It should be **provin-cial**.
10. Words are divided at the end of two successive lines, followed by the division of the final word of the paragraph. This would look better:

   Although we cannot extend credit privileges at the present time, we would be happy to ship merchandise to you on C.O.D. terms. Perhaps in the future, if you try us again, we may be able to reconsider.

CHART III: SPELLING TIPS

There are exceptions to many spelling rules, as you know, but here are some tips that will help you.

Doubling Final Consonants

When the final consonant is preceded by a single vowel and the suffix begins with a vowel, the consonant is doubled. This is true for one-syllable words like *plan* or *run* (*planning, running*) and for multisyllable words that are accented on the last syllable *begin* or *control* (*beginner, controller*).

Dropping the Silent E

A final silent *e* is usually dropped before a suffix beginning with a vowel (*exciting, movable*), but the *e* is retained before a suffix beginning with a consonant (*excitement, movement*).

MIS, DIS, and UN

These prefixes all follow the same formula. They do not become *miss*, *diss*, or *unn* unless the root word begin with *s* or *n*.

> misshapen
> dissatisfy
> unnatural

I Before E

The old rhyme, "*I* before *e* except after *c*," holds true in most words with the *ee* sound. Exceptions include *leisure* and *seize*.

CHART IV: THREE HANDY RULES OF GRAMMAR

Rule 1: WAS/WERE, IS/ARE, WE/US, I/ME

Make your choice by isolating unnecessary words and cutting the sentence down to the bare essentials.

- The *letter* (with its enclosures) *was* mailed yesterday.
- *Each* (of you) *is* expected to cooperate.
- Some of *us* (women) were promoted.

- *We* (women) want equal rights.
- The memorandum was for (Ms. Grimes and) *me*.

Rule 2: HE/HIM, SHE/HER

Reverse the sentence structure to make the correct answer apparent.

- It was *he/him*.
  He was it.
  It was *he*.
- The first to appear were *she/her* and Mr. Forbes.
  She and Mr. Forbes were the first to appear.
  The first to appear were *she* and Mr. Forbes.

Rule 3: WHO/WHOM

The *who/whom* choice can be made in several ways.

1. *Cutting*

- *Who* (shall I say) is calling?

2. *Reversal*

- *Who/whom* do you wish to speak with?
  With *whom* do you wish to speak?
  Whom do you wish to speak with?

3. *Reversal plus substitution of he/she or him/her.*

- *Who/whom* do you wish to assist you?
  Do you wish *her* (*whom*) to assist you?
  Whom do you wish to assist you?

PART III

EFFECTIVE LETTERS

9

Basic Letter-Writing Techniques

You can greatly increase your value as a secretary if you know how to write simple but effective business letters, memos, and reports. The letters you write should be pleasing to the eye and easy to understand. Keep this in mind, whether you type letters yourself or dictate them for transcription by someone else.

9:1 PARAGRAPH DIVISION MADE SIMPLE

A letter always looks better when it is divided into fairly short paragraphs composed of sentences of no more than 20 words.

9:1a The Short Letter

Note how much easier it is to read the following letter when it is divided into shorter paragraphs instead of one forbidding block.

Dear Mr. Perrin:

We sincerely regret the unsatisfactory service you received from one of our repair technicians recently. As a regular customer, you should know that such service is not customary. We carefully select and supervise our employees to make sure that our customers are taken care of efficiently and courteously. When this is not the case, we appreciate having the matter called to our attention. Thank you for taking the time to write to us. We

shall try even harder in the future to give you the kind of service
you expect.

Cordially,

In this second version of the same letter, you will note that
the main subject is contained in the middle paragraph while the
opening and closing thoughts appear in separate paragraphs, with
a more easily readable effect.

Dear Mr. Perrin:

We sincerely regret the unsatisfactory service you received from
one of our repair technicians recently.

As a regular customer, you should know that such service is not
customary. We carefully select and supervise our employees to
make sure that our customers are taken care of efficiently and
courteously. When this is not the case, we appreciate having the
matter called to our attention.

Thank you for taking the time to write to us. We shall try even
harder in the future to give you the kind of service you expect.

Cordially,

9:1b   The Long Letter

In a longer letter the paragraphing becomes a bit more complicated, but there is only one rule to remember. Each paragraph
should cover a single subject or a specific part of a larger topic. In
other words, every time the thought changes, a new paragraph is
required. Try to apply this idea in the following letter.

Dear Ms. Quincy:

Everyone these days is looking for ways to beat inflation. One of
the most effective methods is to order in volume whenever
possible to take advantage of quantity discounts. Our records
show that during the past year you purchased 200 carbon motor
brushes. Since you never ordered more than thirty of these at a
single time, you bought at a higher price than necessary, as
discounts apply only on purchases of fifty or more. In amounts of

fifty, for each order you could have cut your total costs for the year by ten percent. That would have meant considerable savings for you and, if you had ordered in quantities of 100, you could have saved another eight percent. We are always ready to assist customers like you who have good credit, so why not discuss it with one of our representatives? We look forward to hearing from you soon.

Cordially,

Into how many paragraphs would you divide the preceding letter? Five is the correct answer.

The first paragraph gives a general idea of the subject of the letter. The second provides details concerning this particular customer's purchases for the previous year, and the third presents a purchase plan that would save the customer money. The fourth paragraph suggests that the customer take action, and the final paragraph expresses the hope for an early reply. (See the end of this chapter for the corrected letter.)

9:2 KEEPING STATEMENTS POSITIVE

Almost any statement can be written in ether a negative or a positive way. Some people unconsciously fall into the habit of stating things negatively. This habit must be corrected if one is to write effective letters. Notice how much stronger the following sentences are when they are expressed in a positive way.

Negative: If you send us your credit card number and expiration date, we will try to fill your order.

Positive: Please send us your credit card number and expiration date so that we can fill your order promptly.

Negative: I believe you will find our service to be valuable.

Positive: I know you will find our service to be valuable.

Negative: We cannot make delivery on the date you mention.

Positive: We will make delivery as close to the desired date as possible.

Negative: We have very few dissatisfied clients.

Positive: We have many satisfied clients.

In the first example, there are two weak words, *If* and *try*, in the negative statement. These have been eliminated in the positive version. In the second example, the weak word **believe** has been replaced by the stronger **know**. In the third example, the weak word **cannot** has been replaced by the stronger **will**. In the fourth example, the negative word **dissatisfied** has been replaced by the positive word **satisfied**.

Certain words automatically produce a negative reaction. These words include **think, hope, may, might, refuse, delay,** and **impossible**. Words such as **pleasure, convenience, promptly, service, happy, satisfactory,** and **appreciate** induce a more favorable reaction.

9:2a   265 Positive Words

able	declare	favor	handle
absolutely	dedicate	feasible	happy
accommodate	definite	fervent	helpful
advantage	demonstrate	fine	high
agree	dependable	first	idea
alleviate	desire	flair	ideal
amicable	determine	fluent	immense
anticipate	develop	formative	impel
assert	direct	formulate	impetus
assist	distinct	fortify	implement
assure	eager	fortitude	important
bargain	easy	fortunate	improve
basic	efficient	foundation	incentive
beautiful	elated	free	increase
benefit	enable	freedom	indelible
boundless	encourage	fresh	indomitable
brilliant	endeavor	friendly	infallible
broad	enhance	fulfill	infinite
candid	enrich	future	influence
capable	enthusiasm	gainful	ingenious
certain	establish	genuine	inimitable
clear	excellent	gigantic	integrity
compatible	exciting	glamour	intense
concur	expedite	glorious	invaluable
confident	explore	goal	invincible
congratulate	express	grateful	jubilant
cooperate	extraordinary	great	kind
courtesy	facilitate	growth	lasting

legitimate
liberate
liberty
lifelong
like
live
lively
longevity
love
lovely
lucky
lucrative
lustrous
luxury
magical
magnetic
magnificent
magnitude
majesty
major
manageable
manifest
markedly
marvel
marvelous
massive
masterful
matchless
mellow
merit
mettle
might
miracle
modern
momentous
motivation
moving
multiply
munificent

mutual
natural
necessary
negotiate
numerous
nurture
nutrient
objective
oblige
obtain
offer
often
onward
opportune
opportunity
optimism
orderly
original
palatable
palatial
particular
payment
peaceful
perfect
perfectly
permanent
perpetual
persevere
persistence
personality
pertinent
pervading
pleasant
please
pleasure
plentiful
plus
popular
positive

prestige
produce
productive
proficient
propitious
quick
quickly
reasonable
recommend
regular
respect
responsible
restful
revenue
revitalize
revive
reward
safe
safety
salient
salubrious
salutary
sanction
sane
satisfaction
satisfactory
satisfy
scientific
secure
security
shield
significant
smooth
solid
soothing
sparkling
special
spectacular
splendid

spontaneous
standard
steady
strength
stupendous
substantiate
subtle
success
successful
superb
superior
superlative
support
supreme
surely
surmount
surpass
sustaining
sympathy
tenacious
terrific
thank
therapy
thorough
timely
together
total
tranquil
transform
tremendous
trustworthy
uncommon
undoubtedly
unforgettable
unique
unlimited

9:2b Sixty-two Negative Words to Avoid

afraid	fail	misfortune	trouble
anxious	fault	mishandled	unclear
avoid	fear	missing	unfair
bad	hesitate	mistake	unfortunately
cannot	hope	neglect	unpleasant
careless	ignorant	never	unreasonable
claim	ignore	no	unreliable
damage	impossible	not	wait
delay	inadequate	objection	weakness
delinquent	incomplete	poor	will not
deny	inconvenient	problem	wish
difficulty	incorrect	reject	worry
disapprove	injury	sorry	wrong
dissatisfied	insincere	terrible	
error	lacking	trite	
except	loss	trivial	

9:3 THE TRICK OF THE FIVE W'S

Newspaper reporters have one inflexible writing rule, known as *the five W's*. The five W's that every reporter must remember are *who*, *what*, *when*, *where*, and *why*. The writer of a business letter should be equally concrete and specific. Like the reporter, you want to convey the clearest and most complete message in the fewest possible words.

Vague

Dear Sir:

Our sales manager is away from the office and is not expected back for some time.

Meanwhile, I want you to know that your order is being taken care of and will be shipped to you at the earliest possible date.

Please call us if we can be of further service.

Sincerely,

Specific

Dear Mr. Roberts:(**who**)

John Orwell (**who**), our sales manager, is away (**why**) on vacation (**where**) and is not expected back until July 5 (**when**).

Meanwhile, I want you to know that your order of June 15 (**when**) for three model 62 fax machines (**what**) will be shipped to you on June 30 (**when**).

Please call us at 1-800-222-3456 (**where**) if we can be of further service.

Sincerely,

You will note that the specific letter not only deals in concrete facts, names, and dates, but it also sounds more personal. Your company and its clients are not abstractions, but groups of human beings, and you should write a business letter as one person to another, with all the consideration that entails.

9:4 ELIMINATION OF NEEDLESS WORDS

Besides being concrete and specific, the good business letter is simple and direct. Your writing, like your speech, should be free of useless, ineffective words. In the letter that follows, the unnecessary words are underlined. Notice how much better the letter reads without them.

Dear Mr. Carruthers:

Due to the fact that we have recently expanded our operations, we are now in need of new steel shelving for the purpose of storing office supplies. We would like something along the lines of the shelving we purchased from you in the year of 1982.

In the event that you still have this shelving in stock, please send us your catalog and price list in order that we may make a selection.

Thanking you in advance,

Sincerely,

Dear Mr. Carruthers:

Since we have recently expanded our operation, we now need new steel shelving for storing office supplies. We would like something similar to the shelving we purchased from you in 1982.

If you still have this shelving in stock, please send us your catalog and price list so that we may make a selection.

Thank you very much.

Sincerely,

9:5 SIMPLE GUIDE TO EFFECTIVE LETTERS

The most effective letter is one that emphasizes the reader's point of view. When possible, avoid the overuse of *I* and *we*, especially at the beginning of a sentence.

9:5a The YOU Emphasis

Sentences beginning with *I* or *We* can often be restated to begin with *You*.

I/We Emphasis	You Emphasis
We are pleased to inform you . . .	You will be pleased to learn . . .
I would like you to attend . . .	You will no doubt want to attend . . .
We follow this procedure because . . .	You will benefit from this procedure because . . .
We raised $50,000 last year.	You and other contributors donated $50,000 last year.

9.5b A Positive Tone

In addition to the "you" emphasis, you will want your letters to convey a positive tone. This means more than just avoiding negative words and choosing positive ones. It means trying to imagine how you'd feel if you'd received the letter. The tone you choose can make the difference between a good and a poor reaction to your message. Read the following letter and try to determine what makes you feel uncomfortable about how the situation is handled.

Dear Ms. Davies:

We have your letter in which you claim that the typewriter cleaning kit you purchased has not proved satisfactory. You are the first customer to register such a complaint, and we are at a loss to understand it.

We will, however, pick up the package by UPS so that it can be returned to us, if you will let us know the time and day that will be convenient. Also, will you inform us whether you wish to receive a replacement, a credit, or a cash refund?

We are sorry if you were inconvenienced.

Sincerely,

The tone of this letter implies that the reader does not believe the writer's claim and that the writer is somehow to blame for expressing dissatisfaction. The tone also conveys that the company will begrudgingly accept the return of the merchandise, but it seems an inconvenience. The final apology seems insincere.

See if you can determine what makes the tone of the corrected letter more positive.

Dear Ms. Davies:

Thank you for writing to us about the return of your typewriter cleaning kit. We'll be glad to pick it up and to offer you an exchange, credit, or refund.

Please let us know the day and time when we may arrange for UPS to pick up the cleaning kit. Also, if you can supply us with additional information about your typewriter and your cleaning needs, we may be able to suggest an exchange of your kit for one that meet your needs. If you prefer a credit or refund, just let us know.

We look forward to hearing from you.

Sincerely,

In the revised letter, several expressions have been eliminated that contribute to a negative tone:

you claim: suggests a lack of belief

you are the first customer: suggests that the customer's complaint is inappropriate

we are sorry: an insincere apology, not required by the situation

9:5c Openings and Closings

The opening paragraph of any letter should be phrased in such a way that it immediately captures the reader's interest. Depending on the type of letter, the closing paragraph should spur the reader to action or leave the reader with a feeling of reassurance.

Openings: Here are a few sample openings, with examples of how they can be improved.

Dull: We wish to acknowledge receipt of your letter of July 5.

Improved: We have enclosed information about our office products, which you requested in your letter of July 5.

Dull: We have your letter of May 2.

Improved: We have investigated the matter you described to us in your letter of May 2.

Dull: Thank you for your order.

Improved: Than you for your order for six copies of Faulkner's *Sanctuary*.

Dull: We regret that we cannot comply with your request.

Improved: We have given careful consideration to your request.

Dull: Replying to your request . . .

Improved: Thank you very much for your inquiry of December 1.

Dull: Replying to yours of the twelfth . . .

Improved: Thank you for the opportunity to answer your inquiry of November 12.

Closings: Here are a few sample closings, with examples of how they can be improved.

Dull: Hoping to hear from you soon . . .

Improved: Wc look forward to hearing from you when we can be of further service.

Dull: Looking forward to your reply . . .

Improved: We look forward to hearing from you.

Dull:	We enclose a form for your convenience.
Improved:	Please sign and mail the enclosed form.
Dull:	We shall appreciate prompt payment.
Improved:	Please use the enclosed business envelope to mail us your payment of $350.
Dull:	Thanking you, we are . . .
Improved:	Thank you for your interest.
	Thank you for your assistance.
	Thank you for your order.
Dull:	We trust we have been of assistance.
Improved:	Please let us know when we can help again.
Dull:	That is all the information I can give you.
Improved:	The enclosed information describes our products and services.
Dull:	Thank you for writing.
Improved:	Thank you for giving us the opportunity to work with you.

Answer to 9:1b, The Long Letter

Dear Ms. Quincy:

Everyone these days is looking for ways to beat inflation. One of the most effective methods is to order in volume whenever possible to take advantage of quantity discounts.

Our records show that during the past year you purchased 200 carbon motor brushes. Since you never ordered more than thirty of these at a single time, you bought at a higher price than necessary, as discounts apply only on purchases of fifty or more.

In amounts of fifty for each order you could have cut your total costs for the year by ten percent. That would have meant considerable savings for you and, if you had ordered in quantities of 100, you could have saved another eight percent.

We are always ready to assist customers like you, who have good credit, so why not discuss it with one of our representatives?

We look forward to hearing from you soon.

Cordially,

10

Letter Format

First impressions are important, and a letter that is uniform in structure and pleasing to the eye makes the reader more receptive to its contents. Regardless of the format you choose or your company requires, there are seven standard parts of business letters and some optional parts to be used as needed.

10:1   STANDARD PARTS

The standard parts of a letter include

> heading
> date
> inside address
> salutation
> body of letter
> complimentary close
> name and signature

10:1a   Heading

The heading is the printed letterhead stationery your company uses. It contains the information the respondent needs to write a return letter.

10:1b   Date

Type the date two to six lines below the letterhead, and spell out the month. Some companies prefer the international and government style for dates, with the day preceding the month and no punctuation.

6 January 1992

Most American firms use the more familiar month/day/year style:

January 6, 1992

Whichever style you adopt, use the same style in the body of the letter.

10:1c   Inside Address

The inside address should duplicate the name of the firm you are addressing, according to its letterhead or listing in the telephone directory.

Abbreviate or spell out such words as **Company**, **Limited**, and **Incorporated**, to match the firm's official title. A **The** in the title should never be omitted.

Smith Publishing **Co., Inc.**

R.R. Bowker **Company**

Bobley Publishing **Corporation**

The Foundation Press, **Inc.**

W. H. Freeman **& Company**

Use figures for all building numbers except **One**. The building number should not be preceded with **#** or **No.** or a room number.

One Madison Avenue

1124 Broadway

340 Park Avenue, Room 1416

Never:

1 Madison Avenue

#1124 Broadway

No. 340 Park Avenue

Room 1416, 340 Park Avenue

Spell out words that stand for street direction—*South*, *North*, *West*, *East*—except when a line is unusually long or the fastest handling of the mail is required. See standard postal abbreviations for rapid processing by optical character readers, p. 212. Also spell out the names of streets and avenues that are numbered 12 or under.

660 Fifth Avenue

25 West Eighth Street

When figures are used for street names, it is not necessary to add *nd*, *st*, or *th*. You can say "Forty-Second Street," but you would write *East* or *West 42 Street*.

Separate the house number from a numerical street name with a space/hyphen/space to avoid confusion.

1234 - 159 Street

Allow two spaces between the name of the state and the zip code.

Canton, OH   44709

Include the zip code in the letter as well as on the envelope, so you have it for your records.

When an individual in a company is addressed, both the individual name and the company name are included. If there is no street address, the city and state may be placed on separate lines.

Mr. Mark Bentley

Parker Publishing Co., Inc.

West Nyack

New York   10994

Mr., *Mrs.*, *Miss*, or *Ms.* precedes the individual's name, even when a business title is used. The name and title are written on the same line when space permits. Otherwise, they are separated into two lines, or the business title is omitted entirely.

Mr. William W. Durrell, President

Crane Duplicating Service, Inc.

Box 487

Barnstable, MA   02630-7265

Mr. Charles E. Spannaus
Vice President in Charge of Sales
St. John Associates, Inc.
211 West 61 Street
New York, NY   10023

When writing the officer of a company who has several titles, use the title of the higher office, or the office used in the letters which he or she signs.

Ms. Judith Helf, Vice President

or

Ms. Judith Helf, Production Manager
Ahrend Associates, Inc.
64 University Place
New York, NY   10003

The standard form for the inside address is at the top of a letter, rather than at the foot. It should begin no less than two and no more than twelve lines below the date line. If the first line is awkwardly long, it can be carried over and indented two spaces or typed at the left margin.

Automatic Typewritten
    Letters Corporation
151 West 19 Street

10:1d   Salutation

Type the salutation two lines below the inside address, flush with the left-hand margin, and two lines below the attention line, if one is used. Follow the salutation with a colon (or no punctuation).

In most cases you will be addressing an individual, and you should capitalize the first word, the title, and the name. The only titles that should be abbreviated are *Mr., Mrs., Ms.,* and *Dr.*

Dear Mr. Babbett:
Dear Ms. Carin:
Dear Professor Entwood

Never use a business title in a salutation, and never use any title without a surname.

Correct:	Dear Mr. Fordham:
	Dear Professor Graves:
	Dear Dr. Holmes:
Incorrect:	Dear President Fordham:
	Dear Professor:
	Dear Doctor:

Never use an academic degree following a salutation.

Correct:	Dear Mr. Jackson:
	Dear Dr. Jackson:
Incorrect:	Dear Mr. Jackson, M.A.:
	Dear Dr. Jackson, LL.D.

Dear Madam and ***Dear Sir*** are extremely impersonal, as well as outmoded, salutations. It is preferable to use the addressee's name.

Dear Ms. Knight and Mr. Loew:

In less formal business situations, when you're on a first-name basis with the receiver, use his or her first name followed by a colon (or no punctuation).

Dear Mary:
Dear Bob

When you don't know and can't get the name of a particular person to address in your letter, use either the department or group you're addressing or replace the salutation with a subject or attention line.

Dear Customer Service:
Dear Policyholder:
REQUEST FOR INFORMATION ON OFFICE AUTOMATION SYSTEMS
ATTENTION: Marketing Manager

The attention line can take the place of the salutation at the left margin; it can be indented five spaces if the paragraphs are indented; or it can be centered.

Norris Corporation
188 Maple Street
Springfield, MA 01105

Attention: Mr. Owens

Norris Corporation
188 Maple Street
Springfield, MA 01105

    Attention: Mr. Owens

Norris Corporation
188 Maple Street
Springfield, MA 01105

                       Attention: Mr. John Owens

10:1e Body

The body of the letter is single spaced with double spacing (two lines) between paragraphs. For balance, use a minimum of three paragraphs, with the longest paragraph in the middle. One-sentence paragraphs are perfectly appropriate in business letters, especially for first and last paragraphs. Some formats allow for indenting five spaces at the beginning of paragraphs; others do not.

10:1f Complimentary Close

Type the complimentary close two lines beneath the last line of the letter. Most firms now prefer one-word closes. In a two-word close like *Sincerely yours* only the first word is capitalized. All closes are followed by a comma.

    The complimentary close should reflect the formality or informality used in the letter. Popular choices include the following:

Sincerely
Sincerely yours
Cordially
Respectfully
Best wishes
Warmest regards
Regards

10:1g Name and Signature

Type the writer's name and position four lines beneath the complimentary close. Type the writer's position beneath the name, unless the letter is a purely personal one.

The firm's name is usually omitted in the signature of a letter, unless it is a formal document or the writer is speaking legally for the company. When the firm name is used, it is typed two lines below the close, and the writer's name appears four lines below the firm's name. The firm's name should be typed in capitals as it appears on the letterhead. Type signatures exactly as signed by dictators, using initials only where they do. The writer's title follows on the same line or the line below.

Cordially,   Sincerely,

                                        T. TWAIN AND COMPANY

Samuel S. Stone
Vice President

                                        Samuel S. Stone
                                        Vice President

When signing a letter in your own name, as the executive's secretary, precede the executive's name by *Mr.*, *Ms.*, or *Dr.*, and omit initials unless someone else in the firm has the same name.

Sincerely yours,

Secretary to Ms. Williams

If you sign your superior's name to a letter, sign your initials immediately below.

Sincerely,

Bruce Bliven
gp

Bruce Bliven
General Manager

If your superior is a woman and wants to be addressed with a courtesy title other than the standard **Ms.**, you should indicate what form she prefers by placing it in parentheses before her typed name.

(Mrs.) Janet Johnson

If you're typing a letter addressed to a woman, it is correct to address her as Ms. Janet Johnson (See also 11:1b).

10:2 ADDITIONAL PARTS

Additional letter parts are used as needed. Each is separated from the previous part by one double space.

10:2a Addressee Notation

Occasionally a letter will include an addressee notation indicating that it is to be handled in a certain way or that it contains confidential information. Common notations include the following:

PERSONAL
CONFIDENTIAL
PLEASE FORWARD

Such notations are typed two lines above the inside address in capital letters.

10:2b Subject Line

A subject line following the salutation alerts the recipient to the nature of the letter and provides an easy means of filing the letter in the right place. All important words in a subject line are capitalized. The line may be underlined or written in all capital letters. The subject line is never placed before the salutation, as it is part of the body of the letter. It follows the salutation, two lines below it, usually flush with the left-hand margin, although it may be centered. Modern usage often eliminates the word **subject**, and **Re** is outmoded.

Mr. James F. Prentice
New Haven Bank & Trust Company
190 Main Street
New Haven, CT 06502

Dear Mr. Prentice:

Subject: Estate of William Rogers

Mr. James F. Prentice
New Haven Bank & Trust Company
190 Main Street
New Haven, CT 06502

Dear Mr. Prentice:

ESTATE OF WILLIAM ROGERS

Mr. James F. Prentice
New Haven Bank & Trust Company
190 Main Street
New Haven, CT 06502

Dear Mr. Prentice:

Estate of William Rogers

10:2c   Second-Page Heading

When a letter runs longer than one page, an additional heading is required on each page to keep the parts of the letter together if they should become separated. This heading should include the recipient's name, the date of the letter, and the page number. Two formats are acceptable: vertical and horizontal.

Vertical

Ms. Mary Johnson
June 16, 1991
Page 2

Horizontal

Ms. Mary Johnson	-2-	June 16, 1991

Triple space after the second-page heading before continuing the body of the letter.

10:2d   Reference Initials

The dictator's and transcriber's initials are usually typed two lines below the typed name of the signer, although there is no real necessity for it. The signer of the letter is obviously the dictator, unless otherwise indicated, and the transcriber's initials mean nothing to the recipient. For reference purposes, the identification initials place responsibility for the letter's contents on the owners of the initials.

There are a number of ways in which the initials may be typed, according to company policy or the dictator's preference. Assuming that the dictator's initials are **HAD** and the secretary's are **IJ**, these are the various options.

HAD:ij
HAD/ij
HAD:IJ
HAD/IJ
H.A. Dodge: IJ (when dictator's name is not included in typed signature)
KLM:HAD:IJ (when letter is signed by someone other than dictator)
ij (when only the secretary's initials are a matter of record)
IJ

10:2e   Enclosure Notation

If the letter contains an enclosure, the notation appears two lines below the reference initials or previous item. Common forms include the following:

Enclosure
Encl.
Enclosures (2)
Enclosures: Product brochure
Order form

10:2f   Copy Notation

To indicate the names of people receiving copies of the letter, type a copy notation two lines below the enclosure notation or previous item. Common forms include the following:

cc:
CC:
c:

The list should include the name, name and title, or name and address of people receiving the letter. Names are usually listed alphabetically or by rank.

10:3 LETTER STYLES, NEW AND OLD

Choice of overall letter format is up to the department head or individual writer, unless there is a definite company ruling in this regard. No one style is intrinsically superior to another, although the full block style is currently favored.

10:3a Full Block

Full block style has all parts of the letter flush with the left-hand-margin. There is no indentation for the start of each paragraph. Open punctuation is used in the address, with no punctuation except the comma separating city and state, or the comma be-

Full Block

September 12, 19XX

Mr. George J. Nathan
Osgood Advertising Agency
15 Peachtree Street
Atlanta, GA   30332

Dear Mr. Nathan:

Xxxxxxxxxxxxxxx xxxxxxxxxxxxxxx xxxxxxxxxxxxxx
xxxxxxxxxxx xxxxxxxxx xxxxxxx.

Xxxxxxxxxxxxxxxxxx xxxxxxxxxxxxxxxx xxxxxxxxxx
xxxxxxxxxxxxx xxx xxxxxxxxxxxxxxx xxxxxxxxxxxx xxx
xxxxxxxxxxxxxxxxxxxxxx xxxxxxxxxxxxxx xxxxxxxxx
xxxxxxxxxxxxxxxxxx xxxxxxxx xxxxxx xxxxxxx xxxxxxxx
xxxxxxxxx.

Xxxxxxxxxxxxxx xxxxxxxxxxx xxxxxxx xxxxxxxxxxxx
xxxxxxxx xxxxxxxxxxxx xxxxxx xxxxxxxxxx.

Sincerely,

Ruth Stevenson
Advertising Manager

tween a name and title on the same line. Mixed punctuation is generally used for the salutation (a colon) and complimentary close (a comma), although open punctuation (no punctuation) is gaining currency.

10:3b   Modified Block

The modified block style is like the block style with one major change—the date, the complimentary close, and name and signature move to the center or right of center on the page to line up beneath each other. This is the older style, still preferred by some firms since it provides better balance of the letter on the page. However, it does take longer to type since tab settings are required.

Modified Block

September 12, 19XX

Mr. George J. Nathan
Osgood Advertising Agency
15 Peachtree Street
Atlanta, GA   30332

Dear Mr. Nathan:

Xxxxxxxxxxxxxxx xxxxxxxxxxxxxxx xxxxxxxxxxxxxx
xxxxxxxxxxx xxxxxxxxx xxxxxxx.

Xxxxxxxxxxxxxxxxxxx xxxxxxxxxxxxxxxx xxxxxxxxxx
xxxxxxxxxxxxx xxx xxxxxxxxxxxxxxx xxxxxxxxxxxx xxx
xxxxxxxxxxxxxxxxxxxxxxx xxxxxxxxxxxxxx xxxxxxxxx
xxxxxxxxxxxxxxxxx xxxxxxxx xxxxxx xxxxx.

Xxxxxxxxxxxxxx xxxxxxxxxxx xxxxxxx xxxxxxxxxxx
xxxxxxxx xxxxxxxxxxxxx xxxxxx xxxxxxxxxx.

Sincerely,

Ruth Stevenson
Advertising Manager

10:3c   Semiblock

Semiblock is a variation of the modified block style, in which the first line of each paragraph is indented five spaces.

Semiblock

September 12, 19XX

Mr. George J. Nathan
Osgood Advertising Agency
15 Peachtree Street
Atlanta, GA   30332

Dear Mr. Nathan:

Xxxxxxxxxxxxxxx xxxxxxxxxxxxxxxx xxxxxxxxxxxx
xxxxxxxxxxxx xxxxxxxxx xxxxxxx.

Xxxxxxxxxxxxxxxxxxxx xxxxxxxxxxxxxxxx xxxxxxxx
xxxxxxxxxxxxxxx xxx xxxxxxxxxxxxxxxx xxxxxxxxxxxxx xxx
xxxxxxxxxxxxxxxxxxxxxxxx xxxxxxxxxxxxxxx xxxxxxxxx
xxxxxxxxxxxxxxxxxxx xxxxxxxx xxxxxx xxxxxxx xxxxxxxx
xxxxxxxxx.

Xxxxxxxxxxxxxxx xxxxxxxxxxx xxxxxxx xxxxxxxxxxxx
xxxxxxxx xxxxxxxxxxxx xxxxxx xxxxxxxxxx.

Sincerely,

Ruth Stevenson
Advertising Manager

10:3d   Simplified

The Administrative Management Society Simplified, or AMS Simplified, is the newest format and is gaining wide acceptance. It eliminates the salutation and complimentary close. In place of the salutation, the subject line is typed in capital letters. This format works especially well when the addressee's name is not known. When it is known, it is incorporated into the first sentence of the letter. See the example on page 174.

10:4   ENVELOPES

To increase the efficiency of processing mail, the post office has installed Optical Character Readers (OCRs), which require that the name and address be typed on the envelope in a particular

Simplified

February 19, 19XX

Mr. Bruce Chatham, President
Douglas Machinery Corp.
222 Prospect Street
Portland, ME 04105

THE COMPUTER AND YOU

Xxxxxxxxxxxxxxxx xxxxxxxxxxxxxxxx xxxxxxxxxxxxxxx
xxxxxx xxxxxxx xxxxxxxxxxxxxxxxxxxxx xxxxxxxxxx
xxxxxxxxxxxx xxxxxxxxx xxxxxxx.

Xxxxxxxxxxxxxxxxxxxx xxxxxxxxxxxxxxxx xxxxxxxxxxx
xxxxxx xxxxxxxxxxxxxxx xxxxxxxxxxxxxxx xxxxxxxxx
xxxxxxxxxxxxx   xxxxxxxx   xxxxxxxxxxxxxxxxx.

Xxxxxxxxxxxxxxxxxxxxxxxxxxxx.

Ellis F. Grace
Sales Manager

place according to specific requirements. Side margins must be at least 1″ and bottom margins at least ⅝″ but no more than 2¼″. The post office has also requested that firms use the zip + 4 code, which the optical scanners can read. The rules for the OCR are as follows:

1. Keep the left margin flush.
2. Type the city, state, and zip + 4 on the same line.
3. Use the two-letter state abbreviations.
4. Use block letters.
5. Use all capital letters without any punctuation.
6. Place the address as shown below.
7. Provide good contrast between the ink and the paper (black ink on white envelope is the best).
8. When using an address label, be sure that the bottom of the label is parallel with the bottom edge of the envelope.

Quantity mailings and letters that have the highest urgency should comply with these standards. Otherwise, you may want to modify the requirements to use the more widely recognized format of upper- and lowercase letters and commas between the city and state.

Address Area

```
          ┌─────────────────────────────┐
          │                             │
→ 1″ ←    │  NAME OF RECIPIENT          │    ← 1″ →
          │  DELIVERY ADDRESS           │
          │  CITY STATE ZIP + 4         │
          │                             │
          └─────────────────────────────┘
```

Top of last line   ↑
cannot be higher   ⅝″
than 2¼″ from   ↓
bottom of envelope

10:5   SPEED MESSAGES AND INTEROFFICE MEMORANDA

Speed message forms are widely used to save time when a formal letter is not necessary. They are no substitute for a more detailed letter or personal telephone call, but they fill a need to put something down in writing in order to give a quick answer or obtain a fast written reply. Interoffice memoranda serve the same purpose but are designed for use within the organization.

10:5a   Speed Messages

These forms are ruled so the message can be written quickly in longhand if desired, with no salutation or close. A *reply message* enables the recipient to respond immediately on the same form.

Speed messages are usually set up as shown on page 176.

It is a nice touch and contributes to the informality of these messages to precede the signature with *Best wishes* or *Regards*.

10:5b   Interoffice Memoranda

Office memos should be written with as much care as any letters. They should be routed systematically when going to more than one person, either alphabetically, or by location or job priority.

Interoffice or interdivision memos have no salutations or complimentary closes. They can be addressed and signed in either of two ways, as shown on page 177.

SPEED MESSAGE

From
Jason Holmes Co.
217 Eastland Avenue
Detroit, MI 48236
(313) 475-5390

TO _____

SUBJECT _____ DATE _____

_____ Signed _____

REPLY MESSAGE

From
Jason Holmes Co.
217 Eastland Avenue
Detroit, MI 48236
(313) 475-5390

TO _____

SUBJECT _____ DATE _____

Please Reply to _____ Signed

DATE _____ Signed _____
Person Addressed Return This Copy to Sender

DATE: May 7, 1992
TO: Mr. K. Lamson
FROM: Marian Nolan
SUBJECT: Word Processing System Update
(body of memorandum)

or

Mr. K. Lamson
(body of memorandum)
Marian Nolan

When the memorandum is going to several recipients, it is addressed as follows, with an extra copy for each addressee:

TO: Mr. K. Lamson
Ms. May Pierce
Ms. R. Swart

Sometimes a single copy of a memorandum is to go in succession to each person addressed, in which case it is indicated like this:

1. Mr. K. Lamson
2. Ms. M. Pierce
3. Ms. R. Swart

The name of the person writing the memo may be included as number 4 so the memorandum will be returned to the sender.

The letters *FYI* (for your information) are put after the names of persons to whom copies are being sent merely to keep them informed.

10:6   FAX MAIL AND ELECTRONIC MAIL

Facsimile transfer (fax mail) and electronic mail (E-mail) are becoming increasingly common in the modern office. Fax mail requires no special formatting of letters or memos, but it requires that both sender and receiver have a fax machine on a dedicated phone line, which is the fax number.

E-mail requires that the sender and receiver have computer terminals and that both are on the E-mail system. With E-mail systems, the participants must check their "mailboxes" frequently. When used well, E-mail can greatly reduce the number of memos sent. However, since many E-mail messages are printed out and distributed, the same time and attention should be given to composing and typing them as for a letter or memo. Since the typical E-mail screen has fewer lines of type than the standard page, conciseness is critical.

11

Forms of Address

Most business correspondence is addressed to private individuals or corporations, and the forms of address are familiar to the average secretary. Occasions do arise, however, when you must address an official, and you do not want to make a blunder. This chapter deals with such specialized problems and many other questions related to correct modes of address.

11:1 BUSINESS ADDRESS

Although it was once considered proper to address the members of a corporation, company, federation, league, or association as **Gentlemen**, this practice is no longer acceptable because of the increasing numbers of women in business. If you are not writing to a specific person, you have several options to handle the form of address:

1. Call the company to get the name and title of the appropriate person.
2. Use a form of address that designates the department you're addressing.

> Dear Personnel Director:
> Dear Marketing Manager:

3. Use a subject line in place of the salutation.

> Subject: Request for Information About Your Fax Machines

179

4. Use the company or organization as the form of address.

Dear League of Women Voters:

Here, too, it should be noted that even though the title of the organization might suggest an all-female membership, this is not necessarily the case. Therefore, it would be inappropriate to assume that **Dear Ladies** would be correct when writing to an organization like The League of Women Voters.

5. When you don't know the name of the person you're addressing, or you want to use a very generalized form of address, you could resort to the following options:

Dear Ladies and Gentlemen:
Dear Men and Women of Allied Enterprises:

Make sure that when you address both sexes you use terms that are on an equal level, as in the preceding examples. It would be inappropriate, for instance, to address a group as

Dear Gentlemen and Girls:

or

Dear Men and Ladies:

11:1a Male Address

A company official's title is not used in the salutation of the letter.

Mr. William Granville, President
H.L. Mencken Corporation
(local address)

Dear Mr. Granville:

Two individual men addressed simultaneously are addressed in succession by full name, and the higher ranking man is mentioned first. Otherwise, they are listed alphabetically.

Mr. Robert Haines and
Mr. Stuart James
(local address)

Dear Mr. Haines and Mr. James:

11:1b Female Address

The use of **Miss** or **Mrs.** to identify the marital status of women is now less popular than the generic **Ms.** Even the conservative language expert William Safire has finally announced his acceptance of the courtesy title **Ms.**

If a woman prefers that she be addressed as **Mrs.** or **Miss**, she should indicate that in parentheses in front of her name.

- (Mrs.) Mary Johnson

If she doesn't indicate a preference or you're not sure how to address her, choose **Ms.**

Two women are addressed using the courtesy title **Ms.** and giving the name of the woman of superior rank or age first.

- Ms. Mary Thompson and Ms. Beverly Smith

Or you can combine them with the courtesy title **Mses.**

- Mses. Thompson and Smith

If you can't tell from a name whether it's masculine or feminine, you can use the courtesy title **M.** or use the first and last name as the form of address.

- Dear Jackie Johnson:
- Dear M. Johnson:

If you're addressing a married couple with the same last name, the courtesy title is **Mr. and Mrs.** followed by the man's name.

- Mr. and Mrs. Harry Smith

If the couple has different last names, use the courtesy titles **Mr. and Ms.** followed by each person's first and last name.

- Mr. Harry Smith and Ms. Betty Jones

If the wife has a title of superior rank, list her name first.

- Dr. Betty Smith and Mr. John Jones

- Dr. Betty Smith and Mr. John Smith (Dear Dr. and Mr. Smith)

11:1c Doctors and Lawyers

When the signature on a letter is followed by the initials of a doctorate, that means the writer expects to be addressed as **Dr.**

> Katherine Karlin, Ph.D.
> (local address)
>
> Dear Dr. Karlin:
>
> Lawrence Langer, M.D.
> (local address)
>
> Dear Dr. Langer:
>
> Martin Manville, D.D.S.
> (local address)
>
> Dear Dr. Manville:
>
> Norma Mailor, D.V.M.
> (local address)
>
> Dear Dr. Mailor:

You can address a doctor as **Dr. Lawrence Langer**, without the initials, but do not use titles on both ends of a name. **Never** write **Dr. Lawrence Langer, M.D.**

When addressing a doctor and spouse, list the doctor's name first, as **Dr. and Mrs.** or **Dr. and Mr.**

Form of Address	Salutation
Dr. and Mrs. Lawrence Langer	Dear Dr. and Mrs. Langer:
or	
Dr. and Ms. Lawrence Langer	Dear Dr. and Ms. Langer:
or	
Dr. Lawrence and Ms. Mary Langer	Dear Dr. and Ms. Langer:

or

Dr. Katherine and Mr. Philip Karlin   Dear Dr. and Mr. Karlin:

or

(if the doctor's last name is different from her husband's name)

Dr. Katherine Meyers and Mr. Philip Karlin   Dear Dr. Meyers and Mr. Karlin:

Lawyers' titles are mentioned in the address, beneath their names, but they are saluted the same as laypersons.

Mr. Peter Cranshaw
Bailey, Cranshaw, and Daniels
Attorneys at Law
(local address)

Dear Mr. Cranshaw:

Mr. David Erikson
Attorney at Law
(local address)

Dear Mr. Erikson:

Ms. Carol Framish
Attorney at Law
(local address)

Dear Ms. Framish:

11:2 GOVERNMENT OFFICIALS

Honorable is an all-purpose title applicable to most state, local, or federal government officials; but certain personages, like the President, are not addressed that way until they are out of office.

The President and Vice President are never addressed by name.

The President
The White House
Washington, DC 20500

Dear Mr. President:

The Vice President
Dirksen Senate Office Building
Washington, DC 20510

Dear Mr. Vice President:

A former President is known as **Honorable**, unless he also has a military title. He is saluted as **Mr.**

Honorable Chester Alan Arthur
(local address)

Dear Mr. Arthur:

11:2a State and Local

The traditional way of addressing governors and mayors is **Honorable**, but you can address a governor or mayor simply as **Governor** or **Mayor** if you like.

Governors

Honorable Frank Knight
Governor of Colorado
Executive Chambers
Denver, CO 80202

Dear Governor Knight:

Governor Frank Knight
Executive Chambers
Denver, CO 80202

Dear Governor Knight:

The governor of Massachusetts is known as **His** or **Her Excellency**.

His Excellency, the Governor of Massachusetts
State House
Boston, MA 02109

Dear Sir:

Acting governors may be addressed as **Honorable**, but they are saluted as **Mr.**, **Mrs.**, or **Ms.**

Honorable Albert Leonard
Acting Governor of Nevada
Executive Chambers
Carson City, NV 89701

Dear Mr. Leonard:

Lieutenant governors are saluted by title, or as **Mr.**, **Mrs.**, or **Ms.**

Honorable Grace C. Mathews
Lieutenant Governor of Kentucky
Senate Chamber
Frankfort, KY 40601

Dear Lt. Governor Mathews (or Dear Ms. Mathews):

When you do not know a governor's name, address him or her as **The Honorable** plus title. The governor is then saluted as **Dear Sir**, **Dear Madam**, or by title.

The Honorable Governor of Oregon
Executive Chambers
Salem, OR 97301

Dear Sir (or Dear Mr. Governor):

Other State Officials

The state attorney general and secretary of state are addressed as **Honorable** and they are saluted by their official titles.

Honorable Clifford M. Nolan
Attorney General of Texas
State Capitol
Austin, TX 78710

Dear Attorney General Nolan (or Dear Mr. Attorney General):

Honorable David Ottinger
Secretary of State of Texas
State Capitol
Austin, TX 78710

Dear Secretary Ottinger (or Dear Mr. Secretary):

All state senators, including the president of the senate, are saluted as **Dear Senator** or **Dear Mr.**, **Mrs.**, or **Ms.**

Honorable Joseph Palling
President of the Senate of the State of New York
Albany, NY 12224

Dear Senator Palling:

Senator Norman Quigley
New York State Senate
Albany, NY 12224

Dear Mr. Quigley:

All members of the assembly are saluted as ***Dear Assembly-man*** or ***Dear Assemblywoman***. They can also be saluted as ***Dear***, ***Mr.***, ***Mrs.***, or ***Ms***. Representatives or delegates are addressed as ***Honorable*** and are saluted as ***Mr.***, ***Mrs.***, or ***Ms***.

Honorable Paul Rowland
Speaker of the Assembly of the State of New York
Albany, NY 12224

Dear Assemblyman Rowland (or Dear Mr. Rowland):

Assemblywoman Ruth Stevens
Legislative Office Building
Albany, NY 12224

Dear Assemblywoman Stevens:

Honorable Max Steuben
House of Representatives
Montgomery, AL 36104

Dear Mr. Steuben:

The state treasurer, auditor, or comptroller is also called ***Honorable*** and is addressed by the name of the office or as ***Mr.***, ***Mrs.***, or ***Ms***.

Honorable Oscar Thompson
Comptroller of the State of California
State Office Building
Sacramento, CA 95813

Dear Comptroller Thompson (or Dear Mr. Thompson):

Local Officials

The mayor of a city is addressed as *Honorable* or *Mayor* and is saluted as *Mayor*.

Honorable Herbert Vielehr
Mayor of the City of New York
City Hall
New York, NY 10007

Dear Mayor Vielehr:

Mayor Herbert Vielehr
City Hall
New York, NY 10007

Dear Mayor Vielehr:

The president of the Board of Commissioners is addressed and saluted as *Mr.*, *Mrs.*, or *Ms.* or is given the title of *Honorable* and addressed as *President*.

Mr. Isaac Wilder, President
Board of Commissioners of the City of New York
City Hall
New York, NY 10007

Dear Mr. Wilder:

Honorable Isaac Wilder, President
Board of Commissioners of the City of New York
City Hall
New York, NY 10007

Dear President Wilder:

An alderman is addressed as *Alderman* or *Honorable* and saluted as *Mr.*, *Mrs.*, or *Ms.*

Alderman Brian Wilcox (or Honorable Brian Wilcox)
City Hall
Minneapolis, MN 55401

Dear Mr. Wilcox:

A city council member is addressed and saluted as **Councilman** or **Councilwoman** but can also be addressed as **Honorable** and saluted as **Mr.**, **Mrs.**, or **Ms.**

Councilman James Yates
City Council
City Hall
New York, NY 10007

Dear Councilman Yates:

Honorable Jane Yates
City Council
City Hall
New York, NY 10007

Dear Ms. Yates:

11:2b Federal

The President is always addressed as **The President** and **Dear Mr. President**, even when he and his wife are addressed jointly.

The President and Mrs. Adams
The White House
Washington, DC 20500

Dear Mr. President and Mrs. Adams:

If the President were a woman, she would be addressed as **The President** and **Dear Madam President**, even when she and her husband were addressed jointly.

The President and Mr. Adams
The White House
Washington, DC 20500

Dear Madam President and Mr. Adams:

Presidential secretaries are called **Honorable**, with the exception of the press secretary and secretaries who retain military rank.

Honorable Lyle Cantor
Secretary to the President
The White House
Washington, DC 20500

Dear Mr. Cantor:

Honorable Mabel Dodge
Assistant Secretary to the President
The White House
Washington, DC 20500

Dear Mrs. Dodge:

Colonel Philip Eubank
Secretary to the President
The White House
Washington, DC 20500

Dear Colonel Eubank:

Mr. Randolph Fuller
Press Secretary to the President
The White House
Washington, DC 20500

Dear Mr. Fuller:

Cabinet Officers

The attorney general receives the salutation of the office or may be addressed as **Honorable**.

Attorney General Thomas Cartwright (or the Honorable Thomas
Cartwright)
Department of Justice
Constitution Avenue and 10 Street N.W.
Washington, DC 20530

Dear Mr. Attorney General:

Whether other cabinet officers are addressed as **Honorable** is optional. Their salutation is **Dear Mr.** or **Dear Madam Secretary**.

Mr. John Asbury
Secretary of the Treasury
Treasury Department
15 Street and Pennsylvania Avenue N.W.
Washington, DC 20220

Dear Mr. Secretary:

Honorable Jane Brekenridge
Secretary of State
Department of State
2201 C Street, N.W.
Washington, DC 20520

Dear Madam Secretary:

An under secretary may be addressed as **Honorable**, but the salutation includes no title.

Honorable Vernon Devonshire
Under Secretary of Agriculture
Department of Agriculture
14 Street and Independence Avenue S.W.
Washington, DC 20250

Dear Mr. Devonshire:

Members of Congress

Members and former members of the House of Representatives are addressed as **Honorable** or not, as you prefer. The salutation for present members is **Congressman** or **Congresswoman**, and former members are addressed as **Mr.**, **Mrs.**, or **Ms.**

Honorable W. W. Endicott
House of Representatives
Washington, DC 20515

Dear Congressman Endicott:

Representative Alice R. Farrell
House of Representatives
Washington, DC 20515

Dear Congresswoman Farrell:

A resident commissioner or delegate is addressed by title and is saluted as **Mr.**, **Mrs.**, or **Ms.**

Honorable Carla C. Jorges
Resident Commission of Puerto Rico
(or Delegate of Puerto Rico)
House of Representatives
Washington, DC 20515

Dear Ms. Jorges:

The Speaker of the House of Representatives is addressed as
Mr. or **Madam Speaker** but does not retain the title after retiring.

Honorable Edward Hillyer
Speaker of the House of Representatives
Washington, DC 20515

Dear Mr. Speaker (or Dear Mr. or Ms. Hillyer):

Senators, senators-elect, and former senators are addressed
as **Honorable** or not, as you prefer. The title **Senator**, however,
belongs only to one who is presently serving in the Senate.

Honorable D. D. Jellicoe
United States Senate
Washington, DC 20515

Dear Senator Jellicoe:

Senator E. R. Kelland
United States Senate
Washington, DC 20515

Dear Senator Kelland:

Honorable Frances Lewis
Senator-elect
United States Senate
Washington, DC 20515

Dear Mrs. Lewis:

Honorable Giles Monterey
(local address)

Dear Mr. Monterey:

A committee chairman is addressed as **Chairman** and saluted
as **Mr.** or **Madam Chairman**.

Honorable Henry Noble, Chairman
Ways and Means Committee
United States Senate
Washington, DC 20515

Dear Mr. Chairman:

Senator Mary Noble, Chairman
Ways and Means Committee
United States Senate
Washington, DC 20515

Dear Madam Chairman:

Other Federal Officials

The Comptroller General is addressed as such.

Honorable Sidney Nichols
Comptroller General of the United States
Washington, DC 20548

Dear Mr. Nichols:

The Postmaster General is addressed and saluted as such.

Honorable Thomas Cartwright
The Postmaster General
U.S. Postal Service
1200 Pennsylvania Avenue N.W.
Washington, DC 20260

Dear Mr. Postmaster General:

The Librarian of Congress is addressed as such.

Honorable Martha Oppenheim
Librarian of Congress
Washington, DC 20540

Dear Ms. Oppenheim:

Heads or directors of independent agencies are addressed as **Honorable** or **Mr.**, **Mrs.**, and **Ms.** and can be saluted with or without their titles.

Honorable Kurt Pelham, Director
United States Information Agency
1750 Pennsylvania Avenue N.W.
Washington, DC 20547

Dear Mr. Director:

Mr. Joseph C. Rogers, Chairman
Indian Claims Commission
1730 E. Street N.W.
Washington, DC 20006

Dear Chairman Rogers:

Honorable Jane Sutter, Chairman
Civil Service Commission
1900 E. Street N.W.
Washington, DC 20415

Dear Mrs. Sutter:

The head of the Government Printing Office is called the Public Printer and may be addressed as *Honorable*.

Honorable Terence Taylor
Public Printer
Government Printing Office
North Capitol and H Streets N.W.
Washington, DC 20401

Dear Mr. Taylor:

Ambassadors, Ministers, and Consuls

An ambassador is addressed either at his or her embassy in a foreign country or at the State Department in Washington. An ambassador is designated as *Honorable* and is saluted as *Ambassador*.

Honorable Albert Zorach
Ambassador of the United States of America
American Embassy
Moscow, USSR

Dear Mr. Ambassador:

Honorable Shirley Vanderbilt
Ambassador of the United States of America
Department of State
Washington, DC 20520

Dear Madam Ambassador:

Honorable Thomas Wyeth
Ambassador of the United States of America
American Embassy
London, England

Dear Ambassador Wyeth:

Ministers are addressed in care of the U.S. Legations where they are stationed, and they are called *Honorable* or *Excellency*.

Honorable Martin Allen
Legation of the United States of America
Berlin, Germany

Dear Mr. Minister

His Excellency, The American Minister
American Legation
Paris, France

Your Excellency:

An American consul is addressed as *Mr.*, *Mrs.*, or *Ms.* He or she can also be saluted as *Sir* or *Madam*.

Mr. Irving Bliss
American Consulate
Bucharest, Rumania

Dear Mr. Bliss (or Dear Sir):

Ms. Isabel Bliss
American Consulate
Bucharest, Rumania

Dear Ms. Bliss (or Dear Madam):

11:2c   Judicial

The Chief Justice of the U.S. Supreme Court is addressed in either of the following ways:

> The Chief Justice
> The Supreme Court
> Washington, DC 20013
>
> Dear Chief Justice:
>
> Honorable James Stanley
> Chief Justice of the United States
> Washington, DC 20013
>
> Dear Chief Justice:

An associate justice of the U.S. Supreme Court can be addressed in the following ways:

> Justice Edwards
> The Supreme Court
> Washington, DC 20013
>
> Dear Sir (or Madam):
>
> Honorable Albert Edwards
> Associate Justice of the Supreme Court of the United States
> Washington, DC 20013
>
> Dear Justice Edwards:
>
> Honorable Alice Edwards
> Associate Justice of the Supreme Court of the United States
> Washington, DC 20013
>
> Dear Justice Edwards:

A chief justice of a state supreme court is addressed in either of two ways.

> Honorable Barbara Fenway
> Chief Justice of the Supreme Court of New York
> Albany, NY 12207
>
> Dear Madam Chief Justice (or Dear Judge Fenway):

Honorable Basil Fenway
Chief Justice of the Supreme Court of New York
Albany, NY 12207

Dear Mr. Chief Justice (or Dear Judge Fenway):

A retired justice of the U.S. Supreme Court retains an honorary title.

Honorable Christopher Graham
(local address)

Dear Mr. Justice (or Dear Justice Graham):

All other justices and judges are also addressed as **Honorable**.

Honorable Elbert Jenkins
Judge of the United States District Court for the Southern District of
New Jersey
Princeton, NJ 08540

Dear Judge Jenkins:

11:3 EDUCATIONAL OFFICIALS

Whether a full professor is addressed as **Professor** or **Dr.** depends on the possession of the necessary degree and the professor's personal preference.

Professor Frank Oldenberg
(local address)

Dear Professor Oldenberg:

Grace C. Perkins, Ph.D.
(local address)

Dear Dr. Perkins:

Associate or assistant professors are given the same title in the salutation as full professors.

Ms. Diana Martin
Associate (Assistant) Professor
Department of Humanities
(local address)

Dear Professor Martin:

Edward Norris, Ph.D.
Associate (Assistant) Professor
Social Studies Department
(local address)

Dear Dr. Norris:

An instructor is not given a title unless he or she possesses a doctorate.

Mr. Henry Rosen
(local address)

Dear Mr. Rosen:

Isaac Shestov, Ph.D.
(local address)

Dear Dr. Shestov:

Deans and assistant deans get the same salutation, although they may be called *Dr.* in the address.

Dean John C. Thomas
(local address)

Dear Dean Thomas:

Dr. Michael Unger, Dean (Assistant Dean)
(local address)

Dear Dean Unger:

Dean Norma Vanderlyn
(local address)

Dear Dean Vanderlyn:

The president of a college or university receives the salutation of either **Dr.** or **President**.

> Osgood Wynman, L.L.D., Ph.D. (or Dr. Osgood Wyman)
> President, Pace College
> (local address)
>
> Dear Dr. Wyman (or Dear President Wyman):

A college president who is a Catholic priest is addressed as **The Very Reverend** and is saluted as **Father**.

> The Very Reverend Paul Yaeger, President
> Duquesne University
> Pittsburgh, PA 15219
>
> Dear Father Yaeger:

A university chancellor is usually a **Dr.** and is addressed by that title.

> Dr. Brandon Atwood, Chancellor
> University of Hartford
> West Hartford, CT 06107
>
> Dear Dr. Atwood:

High school principals are addressed as **Dr.** if they possess a doctor's degree and indicate it in their correspondence. Otherwise, they are addressed as **Mr.**, **Mrs.**, or **Ms.**

> Dr. George Caldwell, Principal
> Mamaroneck High School
> Mamaroneck, NY 10543
>
> Dear Dr. Caldwell:
>
> George Caldwell, Ph.D.
> Principal, Mamaroneck High School
> Mamaroneck, NY 10543
>
> Dear Dr. Caldwell:

Ms. Harriet Dyer, Principal
Montclair High School
Montclair, NJ 07042

Dear Ms. Dyer:

11:4   MILITARY PERSONNEL

A general's precise rank is designated in the address. All generals
of whatever rank are saluted as *Dear General*.

General of the Army, Donald D. Eisler, U.S.A.
(local address)

Dear General Eisler:

General Edgar Fullbright, U.S.A (or Brigadier General, Lieutenant
General, Major General)
(local address)

Dear General Fullbright:

A colonel or lieutenant colonel receives the salutation of *Colonel*. Rank is indicated in the address.

Colonel (Lieutenant Colonel) Frank Gideon, U.S.A.
(local address)

Dear Colonel Gideon:

An army lieutenant is addressed and saluted in the same way,
whether a first or second lieutenant.

Lieutenant George G. Hollister, U.S.A.
(local address)

Dear Lieutenant Hollister:

Army majors and captains are addressed and saluted by their
titles.

Major Henry Inness, U.S.A.
(local address)

Dear Major Inness:

Captain Isabel Jacobs
(local address)

Dear Captain Jacobs:

An army chaplain is addressed and saluted as *Chaplain*, with the rank of captain following the name in the address. A Catholic chaplain may be saluted as *Father*.

Chaplain James E. Keller, Captain U.S.A.
(local address)

Dear Chaplain Keller:

Chaplain Joseph J. Lowe, Captain U.S.A.
(local address)

Dear Father Lowe:

U.S. Army or Navy warrant officers or flight officers are addressed as *Mr.*, with the initials after their names indicating the branch of service.

Marine Corps titles are the same as those in the Army except that the top rank is *Commandant of the Marine Corps* and the initials *U.S.M.C.* follow the name.

Air Force address is the same as the Army, except that the names are followed by the initials *U.S.A.F.*

Noncommissioned officers in any branch of the service are addressed by their titles, which are also used in the salutation.

Sergeant Joseph Williams, U.S.A.
(local address)

Dear Sergeant Williams:

11:4a   Naval Personnel

Admirals of the Navy must be addressed precisely by their full titles, although all are saluted as *Admiral* or *Dear Sir* (or *Madam*).

Fleet Admiral Manuel N. Norton, U.S.N.
Chief of Naval Operations
Department of the Navy
Washington, DC 20350

Dear Admiral Norton:

Admiral Herbert H. Oppenheim, U.S.N. (or Vice Admiral, Rear Admiral)
(local address)

Dear Admiral Oppenheim:

Commodores are addressed and saluted by their titles.

Commodore Peter J. Quezon, U.S.N.
(local address)

Dear Commodore Quezon:

Commanders are addressed as **Commander** and saluted as **Commander** or **Dear Sir** or **Madam**.

Commander Oliver S. Patton, U.S.N.
(local address)

Dear Commander Patton:

All naval personnel from **Lieutenant Commander** to the lowest rank are addressed and saluted by their titles, although junior officers may be saluted as **Mr.**, **Mrs.**, or **Ms.**

Lieutenant Commander James J. Revlon, U.S.N.
(local address)

Dear Commander Revlon:

Captain Kenneth Southwick, U.S.N.
(local address)

Dear Captain Southwick:

Lieutenant (Lieutenant Junior Grade) Craig L. Trumbull, U.S.N.
(local address)

Dear Mr. Trumbull:

A naval chaplain is addressed as **Chaplain**, with rank following name.

Chaplain Thomas J. Villard, Captain U.S.N.
(local address)

Dear Chaplain Villard:

Coast Guard titles are the same as those in the Navy, except that the top rank is **Admiral** and the initials **U.S.C.G.** are used instead of **U.S.N.**

11:5   RELIGIOUS DIGNITARIES

The pope is addressed as **His Holiness**.

> His Holiness Pope John Paul II
> Vatican City
> State of Italy
>
> Your Holiness (or Most Holy Father):

Other religious dignitaries of the Catholic, Protestant, and Jewish faiths are addressed as follows:

Catholic
An apostolic delegate is addressed as **His Excellency**.

> His Excellency, The Most Reverend Michael Gilroy
> Archbishop of Dublin
> The Apostolic Delegate
> Washington, DC 20013
>
> Your Excellency (or Dear Archbishop Gilroy):

A United States cardinal is addressed as **His Eminence**. His first name is mentioned before the **Cardinal**.

> His Eminence, George Cardinal Hayes
> Archbishop of Chicago
> (local address)
>
> Your Eminence (or Dear Cardinal Hayes):

A Catholic archbishop is addressed as **The Most Reverend** and is saluted as **Your Excellency**.

> The Most Reverend Carl C. Jaeger
> Archbishop of Detroit
> (local address)
>
> Your Excellency:

A Catholic bishop is addressed as ***The Most Reverend*** and is saluted as ***Bishop***.

> The Most Reverend Daniel D. Kroll, D.D.
> Bishop of Boston
> (local address)
>
> Dear Bishop Kroll:

The superior of a community of monks is called an ***abbot*** and is saluted as ***Father***.

> The Right Reverend Adam A. Nelligan
> Abbot of Prinknash Abbey
> Gloucester, England
>
> Dear Father Abbot (or Dear Father Nelligan):

A cleric belonging to the staff of a cathedral is called a ***canon*** and is saluted by that title.

> The Reverend Francis F. O'Boyle
> Canon of Washington Cathedral
> (local address)
>
> Dear Canon O'Boyle:

A monsignor is addressed as ***The Right Reverend*** if he is a local prelate, and ***The Very Reverend*** if he is a papal chamberlain.

> The Right Reverend Monsignor John J. Phillips
> (local address)
>
> Right Reverend Monsignor Phillips:

A monk is addressed as ***Brother***; a nun is addressed as ***Sister***.

> Brother Elias E. Rodgers
> (local address)
>
> Dear Brother Rodgers:
>
> Sister Maria Theresa
> (local address)
>
> Dear Sister Maria Theresa:

A mother superior is addressed as **The Reverend Mother**, followed by the initials of her order.

The Reverend Mother Superior, O.C.A.
(local address)

Dear Reverend Mother (or Dear Mother Superior):

A sister superior is addressed as **The Reverend Sister** and is saluted as **Sister Superior**.

The Reverend Sister Superior
(local address)

Dear Sister Superior:

A superior of a brotherhood is addressed as **The Very Reverend**, followed by the initials of his order. He is saluted as **Father Superior**.

The Very Reverend Joseph Todd, S.F., Director
Monastery of the Franciscan Friars
(local address)

Dear Father Superior:

A Catholic priest with a doctorate is saluted as **Dr.** Otherwise, he is called **Father**.

The Reverend Kenneth Venable, Ph.D.
(local address)

Dear Dr. Venable:

The Reverend Lawrence Wylie
(local address)

Dear Father Wylie:

Protestant
A Protestant archbishop is addressed as **His Grace**.

His Grace
The Lord Archbishop of Canterbury
Canterbury, England

Your Grace (or My Lord Archbishop):

Most other Protestant bishops are addressed as **Bishop** or **The Reverend**. If they hold a doctor's degree, you may use **Dr.**

Bishop Bruce B. Lee, D.D.
(local address)

Dear Bishop Lee:

The Reverend Bruce B. Lee, D.D.
(local address)

Dear Dr. Lee:

A Protestant Episcopal bishop is addressed as **The Right Reverend**.

The Right Reverend John Gifford, D.D.
Bishop of Phoenix
(local address)

Right Reverend Sir (or Dear Bishop Gifford):

An Episcopal priest with a doctor's degree is addressed as **Dr.** Otherwise, use **Mr.** or **Father** for a man, and **Mrs.** or **Ms.** for a woman.

The Reverend Saul Ackerman, D.D., Litt.D.
(local address)

Dear Dr. Ackerman (or Dear Father Ackerman):

The Reverend Saul Ackerman
(local address)

Dear Mr. Ackerman (or Dear Father Ackerman):

The Reverend Victoria Benson, D.D.
(local address)

Dear Dr. Benson:

The Reverend Victoria Benson
(local address)

Dear Mrs. Benson:

A Protestant minister with a doctor's degree is saluted as *Dr.* Otherwise, use *Mr.*, *Mrs.*, *Ms.*, or *Pastor.*

> The Reverend David Chase, D.D.
> (local address)

> Dear Dr. Chase:

> The Reverend David Chase
> (local address)

> Dear Mr. Chase (or Dear Pastor Chase):

> The Reverend Dorothy Chisholm
> (local address)

> Dear Ms. Chisholm:

Jewish

A rabbi is addressed as *Rabbi* unless he or she possesses a doctor's degree. In that case, the salutation is *Doctor.*

> Rabbi Susan Dietrich, Litt.D.
> (local address)

> Dear Dr. Dietrich:

> Rabbi Morris Loeb
> (local address)

> Dear Rabbi Loeb:

11:6 FOREIGN AND U.N. ADDRESS

A foreign ambassador in the United States is addressed as *His* or *Her Excellency* and is saluted as *Excellency* or *Mr.* or *Madam Ambassador.*

> His Excellency, Arthur A. Karlson
> Ambassador of Sweden
> Washington, DC 20027

> Dear Mr. Ambassador:

A foreign chargé d'affaires in the United States is addressed as *Mr.*, *Mrs.*, or *Ms.*

Mr. José J. Rodriguez
Chargé d'Affaires of Chile
Washington, DC 20027

Dear Mr. Rodriguez:

A foreign minister in the United States is addressed as *The Honorable* and is saluted as *Mr.* or *Madam Minister*.

The Honorable Lance duLac
Minister of France
Washington, DC 20027

Dear Mr. Minister:

A foreign ambassador to the United Nations is addressed as *His* or *Her Excellency* and is saluted as *Excellency* or *Mr.* or *Madam Ambassador*.

His Excellency, Curtis C. Cabot
Representative of Canada to the United Nations
New York, NY 10017

Dear Mr. Ambassador:

A United States ambassador to the United Nations is addressed as *The Honorable* and is saluted as *Mr.* or *Madam Ambassador*.

The Honorable Shirley Black
United States Representative to the United Nations
New York, NY 10017

Dear Madam Ambassador:

A United States representative to the United Nations is addressed as *The Honorable* and is saluted as *Mr.*, *Mrs.*, or *Ms.*

The Honorable Gerald G. Gould
Senior Representative of the United States
to the General Assembly of the United Nations
New York, NY 10017

Dear Mr. Gould:

The Secretary General of the United States is addressed as *His* or *Her Excellency* and is saluted as *Excellency* or *Mr.* or *Madam Secretary General*.

His Excellency, Arthur A. Andrews
Secretary General of the United Nations
New York, NY 10017

Dear Mr. Secretary General:

12

Abbreviations

In a business letter, it shows poor taste to abbreviate ordinary words like *received*, *department*, or *months*, even though your correspondent will know the meaning of *rec'd.*, *dept.*, and *mo.* There are, however, many words that are abbreviated by custom, like *Mister (Mr.)*, *post meridiem (P.M.)*, and *cash on delivery (C.O.D.)*. In addition, abbreviations like NATO, OPEC, and ICBM have become part of our current language.

12:1 WHERE TO AVOID ABBREVIATIONS

1. Do not abbreviate the name of a month, even in the heading of a letter.

September 14, 199–
Your letter of January 4

2. Do not abbreviate titles when used with a last name only.

Senator Johnson
Reverend Smith
Professor Jones

Abbreviations may be used before full names or before initials with last names.

209

Rev. Cecil Connelly
Sen. Elbert Keane
Professor G. Eliot
Col. Frank Field
Capt. E. W. Evans

3. Do not abbreviate first names of persons unless they do so in their signatures.

Frederick M. Foster *not* Fred M. Foster

4. Avoid colloquial abbreviations like *lab* for *laboratory*, *info* for *information*, and *steno* for *stenographer* or *stenography*.

5. Abbreviations like *Co.* for *company*, and *No.* for *number*, are permissible in combination with other terms, but not when used alone.

You have a **number** of models to choose from.
This is our model **No.** 1234.
You are invited to the **company** outing.
We purchased the material from J. Jones & **Co.**

12:2 MEASUREMENTS—NEW METRIC AND U.S. STANDARD

Measurements of any kind are not abbreviated in the body of a letter, but in orders or invoices and lists or tables they may be abbreviated to save time and space.

Metric System

LENGTH	kilometer	km
	hectometer	hm
	decameter	dam
	meter	m
	decimeter	dm
	centimeter	cm
	millimeter	mm
AREA	square kilometer	km^2
	hectare	ha
	are	a

	centare	ca
	square centimeter	cm²
	square meter	m²
MASS &	metric ton	mt **or** T
WEIGHT	quintal	q
	kilogram	kg
	hectogram	hg
	decagram	dag
	gram	g
	decigram	dg
	centigram	cg
	milligram	mg
VOLUME	cubic centimeter	cc **or** cm³
	stere	s
CAPACITY	kiloliter	kl
	hectoliter	hl
	decaliter	dal
	liter	l
	deciliter	dl
	centiliter	cl
	milliliter	ml
TEMPERATURE	Celsius	C
	centigrade	c

U.S. Standard

LENGTH	mile	mi.
	rod	rd.
	yard	yd
	foot	ft **or** '
	inch	in. **or** in **or** "
	square mile	sq. mi. **or** mi.²
	acre	a. **or** A
	square rod	sq. rd. **or** rd.²
	square foot	sq. ft. **or** ft²
	square inch	sq. in. **or** in²
VOLUME	cubic yard	cu. yd. **or** yd³
	cubic foot	cu. ft. **or** ft³
	cubic inch	cu. in. **or** in³
WEIGHT	ton	tn.
	hundredweight	cwt.

	pound	lb.
	ounce	oz. **or** oz
	dram	dr.
	grain	gr.
CAPACITY	barrel	bbl. **or** bbl
(LIQUID)	gallon	gal.
	quart	qt.
	pint	pt.
	gill	gi.
	fluid ounce	fl. oz.
	fluid dram	fl. dr.
CAPACITY	bushel	bu. **or** bu
(DRY)	peck	pk. **or** pk
	quart	qt. **or** qt
	pint	pt.
TEMPERATURE	Fahrenheit	F

12:3 LATEST POSTAL ABBREVIATIONS

In the address of a letter, it is customary to write out such words as *avenue*, *street*, *square*, or *place*. The abbreviations *NW*, *SW*, *NE*, and *SE* are used to indicate sections of cities, but the words *North*, *South*, *East*, and *West* are customarily spelled out, as well as the words *county*, *fort*, *mount*, *point*, and *port*.

The name of a city, no matter how long, should not be abbreviated except for use on addressing equipment, in which case you can write, for example, *Prt Jefferson* or *Pt Chautauqua*. These spellings must follow the regulations of the U.S. Postal Department, as no other special abbreviations are permitted. You cannot write *Va. Beach* if the Post Office abbreviates it as *Virginia Bch*.

Common abbreviations now recommended by the post office for quick reading by the Optical Character Readers (high-speed equipment used to speed mail processing) include the following:

Ave. (AVE)
Blvd. (BLVD)
Cir. (CIR)
Ct. (CT)
Expy. (EXPY)
St. (ST)

Tpke. (TPKE)
Ln. (LN)
Pky. (PKY)
Rd. (RD)
Sq. (SQ)
N
S
E
W

A list of all such permissible abbreviations may be obtained from the Post Office Department in Washington, DC.

12:3a   State and Territory Abbreviations

The traditional state abbreviations, like **Conn.** for **Connecticut** and **Ala.** for **Alabama**, have been replaced by two-letter postal abbreviations. These postal abbreviations for states, territories, and possessions of the United States allow computer files to be standardized, requiring only two spaces for each entry. The standardized format allows Optical Character Readers (OCRs) to process the mail much more quickly.

Alabama	AL
Alaska	AK
American Samoa	AS
Arizona	AZ
Arkansas	AR
California	CA
Canal Zones	CZ
Colorado	CO
Connecticut	CT
Delaware	DE
District of Columbia	DC
Florida	FL
Georgia	GA
Guam	GU
Hawaii	HI
Idaho	ID
Illinois	IL

Indiana	IN
Iowa	IA
Kansas	KS
Kentucky	KY
Louisiana	LA
Maine	ME
Maryland	MD
Massachusetts	MA
Michigan	MI
Minnesota	MN
Mississippi	MS
Missouri	MO
Montana	MT
Nebraska	NE
Nevada	NV
New Hampshire	NH
New Jersey	NJ
New Mexico	NM
New York	NY
North Carolina	NC
North Dakota	ND
Ohio	OH
Oklahoma	OK
Oregon	OR
Pennsylvania	PA
Puerto Rico	PR
Rhode Island	RI
South Carolina	SC
South Dakota	SD
Tennessee	TN
Texas	TX
Trust Territories	TT
Utah	UT
Vermont	VT
Virginia	VA
Virgin Islands	VI
Washington	WA
West Virginia	WV
Wisconsin	WI
Wyoming	WY

12:3b   Canadian Abbreviations

Alberta	AB
British Columbia	BC
Labrador	LB
Manitoba	MB
New Brunswick	NB
Newfoundland	NF
Northwest Territories	NT
Nova Scotia	NS
Ontario	ON
Prince Edward Island	PE
Quebec	PQ
Saskatchewan	SK
Yukon Territory	YT

12:4   BUSINESS AND TECHNICAL TERMS

Avoid abbreviations whenever possible, but when you must use them, the following are standard:

A

abridged	abr.
account current	a/c
account of	a/o
accounts payable	AP, A/P
accounts receivable	AR, A/R
actual weight	A/W
additional premium	a.p.
ad infinitum	ad inf.
ad libitum	ad lib.
ad locum	ad loc.
administration	admin.
administrator	adm.
ad valorem	a.v., a/v
advertisement	advt., ad
affidavit	afft.
affirmed	aff'd
after date	a/d
afternoon (post meridiem)	p.m. or P.M.

against all risks	a.a.r.
agent, agreement	agt.
a good brand	a.g.b.
all risks	A/R
alternating current	A.C.
amended	amd.
American terms	A/T
American wire gauge	A.W.G.
amount	amt.
ampere(s)	amp
ampere-hours	amp hr.
amplitude modulation	AM, am
angstrom unit(s)	Å
anonymous	anon.
answer, answered	ans.
approved	appd.
approximately	approx.
arrival, arrived	arr.
article	art.
assessment	assmt.
assessment paid	Apd.
assignment	assigt.
assistant	asst.
association	assn., ass'n
as soon as possible	ASAP
at (price)	@
atomic weight	at. wt.
at sight	a.s.
attached to other corres.	A. to O.C.
attorney	atty.
audio frequency	AF
authorized version	A.V., AV
average	av.

B

bail bond	b.b.
balance	bal.
bank	bk.
bank draft	BD
bank post bill	b.p.b.

bankrupt	bkpt.
barometer	bar.
barrel(s)	bbl., bbl
basket(s)	bsk.
before Christ	B.C.
before noon (ante meridiem)	a.m.
bibliography	bibliog.
bill of collection	B/C
bill of entry	B/E
bill of exchange	B/E
bill of health	B/H
bill of lading	B/L
bill of parcels	B/P
bill of sale	B/S, BS
bill of sight	B/St.
billion electron volts	BeV
bills payable	B/P, BP
bills receivable	B/R
biography	biog.
biology	biol.
board feet	bd. ft.
bonded goods	B/G
book value	b/v
boulevard	blvd., boul.
box	bx.
brake horsepower	bhp, b.hp
British thermal unit(s)	Btu
brother	Bro.
brothers	Bros.
brought over	b/o
building	bldg.
bulletin	bul., bull.
business	bus.
business manager	bus. mgr.
buyer's option, back order	b.o.

C

candlepower	cp
capital	cap.
capital account	C/A

capital letters	caps
carat	K., kt.
carload	c.l.
carriage paid	cge. pd.
carried down	c/d
carried forward	C/F
carried over	c.o.
carrier's risk	C.R.
cartage	ctge., ctg.
case(s)	c., C., Cs.
cash before delivery	C.B.D.
cash book	C/B
cash letter	C/L
cash on delivery	C.O.D., COD
cash on shipment	C.O.S., COS
cash order	C.O.
cash with order	c.w.o.
cask(s)	ck.
cent(s)	c.
Central Standard Time	C.S.T., CST
Central Time	C.T., CT
certificate(s) of deposit	C/D, CD
certificate of origin	C/O
Certified Public Accountant	C.P.A., CPA
chapter (law citations)	c., C.
chapter(s)	ch., chap.
Chartered Accountant	C.A., c.a.
check	ck.
chief value	c.v.
civil	civ.
collateral trust	coll. tr., cit.
collection and delivery	c.&d.
commercial dock	C/D
commercial weight	C.W.
Commissioner, Commission	Comm.
Committee	Comm.
company's risk	C.R.
company, county	co.
consignment	C/N, consgt.

consular invoice	C.I.
cooperative	co-op
copy to	c.c., cc, CC
corporation	corp.
cost and freight	C.A.F., c.f., C.F.
cost, assurance, and freight	c.a.f.
cost, freight, and insurance	c.f.i., C.F.I.
cost, insurance, and freight	c.i.f., C.I.F.
craft loss	c/l
credit, creditor	cr.
credit note	C/N
cumulative	cum.
cumulative preferred	cu. pf., cum. pref.
current, currency	cur.
current account	c/a

D

daily and weekly till forbidden	d.&w.t.f.
day book	DB, D.B.
days after acceptance	d/a
days after date	D/d
days after sight	D/s
dead freight	d.f.
dead weight	DW
dead weight capacity	DWC
debenture	deb.
debenture rights	db. rts.
debit, debtor	dr.
debit note	D/N
decibel	dB
decision	dec.
deferred	def.
delivered	dld.
delivered at destination	dd.
delivered out of ship	ex ship
delivery order	D/O
demand draft	D.D.
demand loan	D/L
department	dept.

deposit account	DA
deposit certificates	dep. ctfs.
deposit receipt	D/R
depreciation	depr.
deviation clause	D/C
diameter	diam, dia.
died	ob.
direct current	DC, dc
director	dir.
direct port	d.p.
discount	dis.
dispatch loading only	d.l.o.
district	dist.
ditto	do.
dividend, division	div.
division freight agent	D.F.A.
dock warrant	D/W
documents against payment	D/P
dozen	doz.
draft	dft.
drawback	dbk.

E

each	ea.
Eastern Daylight Savings Time	E.D.T., EDT
Eastern Standard Time	E.S.T., EST
editor, edition(s)	ed.
editorial note	Ed. Note
effective, efficiency	eff.
electric	elec.
electrostatic unit	esu
empty	m.t.
enclose, enclosed, enclosure	enc., encl.
encyclopedia	encycl., encyc., ency.
end of month	e.o.m.
endorse, endorsement	end.
engineer, engine, engraved	eng.
equipment	equip.
errors and omissions excepted	E.&O.E.

errors excepted	e.e.
estate, estimate, established	est.
et alii (and others)	et al.
et cetera (and so forth)	etc.
except as otherwise noted	E.A.O.N.
except as otherwise herein provided	e.o.h.p.
exchange bill of lading	Ex.B.L.
ex coupon	ex/cp, x-cp.
ex dividend	ex div. x-div.
executive	exec.
executor	exr.
ex interest	ex int., x-int.
ex new	ex-n.
ex officio	e.o.
express, expenses, export	exp.
ex privileges	x-pr.
ex rights	ex r., x-rts.
extraordinary session	extra. sess.
ex warrants	xw

F

facsimile	fac.
fascimile transfer	fax
fair average quality	FAQ
fair average quality of season	FAQS
fast as can	f.a.c.
fathom(s), from	fm.
feet board measure	fbm.
feet per minute	f.p.m., fpm
feet per second	f.p.s., fps
figure(s)	fig(s).
fire risk on freight	f.r.o.f.
firm offer	F.O.
first class	A-1
floating policy, fully paid	F.P.
folio, following	fol., ff.
foreign exchange	FX
for example (exempli gratia)	e.g.
forward	fwd.

for your information	FYI
free delivery	f.d.
free from alongside, free foreign agency	f.f.a.
free of damage	f.o.d.
free of income tax, free in truck	f.i.t.
free on board	f.o.b.
free on field	f.o.f.
free on quay	f.o.q.
free on rail	f.o.r.
free on steamer	f.o.s.
free on truck	f.o.t.
free overside	F.O.
freight	frt.
freight and demurrage	f.&d.
freight bill	F.B.
freight release	F/R
fresh water damage	f.w.d.
frequency modulation	FM, fm
full interest admitted	f.i.a.
full terms	f.t.

G

gallons per minute	g.p.m.
general average	G.A.
general freight agent	G.F.A.
general passenger agent	G.P.A.
good fair average	g.f.a.
good this month	G.T.M.
good this week	G.T.W.
good till canceled	G.T.C.
government	govt.
gross	gro.
gross weight	gr. wt.
guaranteed	guar.

H

handkerchief(s)	hdkf.
hardware	hdwr.

head	hd.
held covered	H.C.
high water, hot water	HW
high-water mark	HWM
high-water ordinary spring tide	H.W.O.S.T.
hogshead(s)	hhd.
hold for money	H.F.M.
horsepower	hp
hour(s)	hr
hypothesis	hyp., hypoth.

I

id est (that is)	i.e.
idem (the same)	id.
incorporated	Inc., inc.
increased value, invoice value	i.v.
indicated horsepower	i.h.p., ihp
institute, institution, instant	inst.
intelligence quotient	IQ, I.Q.
interest, interior	int.
Internal Revenue Service	IRS
International News Service	INS
in the same place (ibidem)	ibid., ib.
invoice, invention	inv.
invoice book, inwards	I.B.I.
invoice book, outwards	I.B.O.
italics	ital.

J

joint account	JA
joint stock	jnt. stk.
joule, current density	J
journal, journalist	jour.
Judge, Justice	J.
Judge Advocate	J.A., JA
Justice of the Peace	J.P., JP
Justices, Judges	J.J.
juvenile	juv.

K

kilocycle(s)	kc
kilovolts	kv
kilowatt(s)	kW
kilowatt-hour(s)	kWh
knocked down	K.D.
knot	k.

L

landing account	L/A
landing and delivery	ldg. & dely.
large	lge., lg.
latitude	lat.
Lawyers Edition	L. ED.
leakage and breakage	Lkg. & Bkg.
leave	lv.
less-than-carload lot	LCL
let me see correspondence	L.M.S.C.
letter of authority	L/A
letter of credit	L/C
life insurance policy	L.I.P.
light vessel	Lt. V.
limited	Ltd.
lire	l.
listed	L
loading	ldg.
loads	lds.
loco citato (in the place cited)	loc. cit.
logarithm	log.
longitude	long.
long ton	l.t.
lower case	l.c., lc
low water	LW
low-water mark	LWM

M

main hatch	M.H.
manager	mgr.

manufacturer	mfr.
manufacturing	mfg.
manuscript(s)	ms(s)., ms(s), MS(s)
margin	marg.
marginal credit	M/C
marine insurance policy	M.I.P.
marked capacity	mc.
marked value	m.v.
married, male	m.
master of ceremonies	M.C., m.c.
mathematics, mathematical	math.
maximum	max.
maximum capacity	max. cap.
mean effective pressure	m.e.p., mep
measurement	mst.
megacycle	Mc
megaton	mt
memorandum(s)	memo(s)
memorandum of deposit	M/D
merchandise	mdse.
miles per hour	m.p.h., mph
minimum bill of lading	min. B/L
minute(s)	min., min(s)
miscellaneous	misc.
money order	M.O., MO
month(s)	mo., mos.
months after date	m/d
months after sight	m/s
morning (anti meridiem)	A.M., a.m.
mortgage certificate coupon	mt. ct. cp.
mountain	mt., mtn.
Mountain Standard Time	M.S.T., MST
my account	m/a

N

national	natl., nat.
nautical	naut.
net proceeds	n/p
net register	n.r.

net tons, new terms	n.t.
net weight	nt. wt.
new charter	N/C
New England	N.E.
night message	N.M.
no account	n/a
no advice	N/A
no date	N.D., n.d.
no effects	N/E
no funds	n/f
no good	N.G., NG
nolle prosequi	nol. pros.
no mark	n/m
nominal horsepower	N.H.P.
nominal standard	nom. std.
nominative	nom.
non sequitur	non. seq.
nonpersonal liability	N.P.L.
nonvoting	n.v.
no orders	N/O
no protest, notary public	N.P.
no risk	n.r.
no risk after discharge	n.r.a.d
note well (nota bene)	n.b., N.B.
not elsewhere specified	n.e.s.
not otherwise enumerated	N.O.E.
not otherwise herein provided	N.O.H.P.
not otherwise specified	n.o.s.
not sufficient funds	N.S.F., n.s.f.
number	No., no.

O

ocean and rail	o.&r.
obsolete, obscure	obs.
official interpretation	off. interp.
Old English	OE, O.E.
Old Series	o.s.
old terms, on truck	o/t
on account of, on or about	o/a

on demand, overdraft	o/d
one way	ow
on sample, on sale	O/S
open charter, old charter, overcharge	o/c
open policy	O.P.
opinion, out of print	op., op
order bill of lading	O.B./L, ob/l
order of	O/o
out of stock	o/s
over, short, and damaged	o.s.&d.
owner's risk	o.r.

P

Pacific Standard Time	P.S.T., PST
Pacific Time	P.T., PT
package	pkg., pkge.
packed weight	p.w.
page	p.
pages	pp.
pair, price	pr.
pamphlet	pam.
parcel post	P.P., p.p.
partial loss	p.l.
participating	part.
particular average	P/Av.
passed, paid	pd.
patent	pat.
pay on delivery	P.O.D.
payable on receipt	P.O.R.
pennyweight	pwt.
per annum (by the year)	p.a.
percent	p.c., pct.
pier diem (per day)	p.d., P.D.
place of the seal	L.S.
please exchange	P.X.
port dues, police department	P.D.
post office	PO, p.o.
postscript	P.S., p.s.
power of attorney, purchasing agent	P/A

preface	pref.
preferred	pfd.
premium	pm.
prepaid, post paid	ppd.
price current, petty cash	P/C, p/c
principal	prin.
private branch exchange	P.B.X., PBX
professional corporation	P.C.
profit and loss	P.&L.
promissory note	P/N, p.n.
prompt loading	ppt.
protection and indemnity	p.&i.
pro tempore	pro. tem.
proximate, proximo	prox.
public address system	PA
public sale	P/S
put and call	P.A.C.

Q

quality	qlty.
quantity discount agreement	q.d.a
quarter	qr.
question, query	q.
questions, queries	qq.
quod erat demonstrandum (which was to be demonstrated)	Q.E.D.
quod vide (which see)	q.v.

R

radio frequency	r.f.
rail and lake	r.&l.
rail and ocean	r.&o.
rail, lake, and rail	r.l.&r.
railroad	R.R., RR
railway	ry., rwy.
real estate	R.E., RE
ream, room(s)	rm.
receipt of goods	R.O.G.
received	recd., rec'd.

referee, reference	ref.
refer to acceptor	R/A
refer to drawer	R/D
refund	rf.
regarding	re
registered, regulation	reg.
regular session	reg. sess.
reinsurance	R.I.
report	rep., rept.
residue, resident	res.
répondez s'il vous plaît (please reply)	R.S.V.P., r.s.v.p.
returned	retd.
return of post for orders	R/p
return premium	R.P.
revenue account	rev. A/C
reversed	rev.
reversing	revg.
revolutions per minute	r.p.m., rpm
revolutions per second	r.p.s., rps
rotation number	rotn. no.
running days	r.d.
Rural Free Delivery	R.F.D., RFD

S

sack(s)	sk.
safe arrival	s/a
Saint	St.
salvage charges	S.C.
salvage loss	s.l.
secretary	secy., sec.
section(s)	sec.
seller 7, 10, 15 days to deliver	s7d, s10d, s15d
seller's option, strike out	s.o.
shaft horsepower	shp, s.hp.
share, sheet	sh.
shipment	shpt.
shipowner's liability	S.O.L.
shipper and carrier	s.&c.
shipper's weights, southwest	S.W.

shipping note	S/N
sight draft, bill of lading attached	S.D.B.L., SD B/L
signed	sgd.
sine die (indefinitely)	s.d.
sinking fund	S.F.
so, thus	sic
society, social	soc.
solicitor(s), solution	sol.
Solicitor's Opinion	Sol. Op.
special opinion	sp. op.
special term	sp. term
standard	std.
standard wire gauge	S.W.G.
statement of billing	S/B
station, stationary	sta.
station to station	S. to S.
statute(s)	stat.
steamer, steamship	str., S.S., SS
sterling	stg.
stock	stk.
stopping in transit	s.i.t.
subject to approval	s/a
subject to approval no risk	s.a.n.r.
superintendent	supt., Supt., super.
supplement	supp.

T

telegram, telegraph, telephone	tel.
telegraphic transfer	TT
territory	ty., ter.
thousand	M
till forbidden	tf, t.f.
time deposits	T/D
timed wire service	TWS
time loan	T/L
tons registered	T.R.
total loss only	t.l.o.
township	twp
trade expenses	T.E.

Traffic Agent	T.A.
transmit	TR
translated, transportation	trans.
transpose	tr.
treasurer	treas.
trial balance	t.b.
trust receipt	T/R

U

ultimo, ultimate	ult.
ultra high frequency	UHF, uhf
underwriter	UW
underwriting account	U/A
United Parcel Service	UPS
United Press	UP
university	univ., U.
until countermanded	T/C

V

valuation clause	V.C.
value-added tax	VAT
versus	vs.
very high frequency	VHF, vhf
vice versa	v.v.
videlicet (namely)	viz.
video frequency	V.F., VF
volume	vol.

W

warehouse receipt	W.R.
warehouse warrant	W/W
warranted	w/d
water and rail	w.&r.
waterproof paper packing	w.p.p.
wavelength	w.l.
week, work	wk.
weight	wt.
weight and/or measurement	W/M

weight guaranteed, wire gauge	w.g.
when issued	w.i.
wholesale	whsle.
with warrants	W.W., ww
without prejudice	w/p, WP
words per minute	w.p.m., wpm

Y

yard	yd.
year, your	yr.
yearbook	yb.

Z

zero, population growth	ZPG
zone, zero	z.
zoology, zoological	zool.

12:5 ASSOCIATIONS, AGENCIES, ORGANIZATIONS, AND OTHER ABBREVIATIONS

Some abbreviations are so widely used and understood that it is perfectly proper to use them in the body of a letter. Everyone knows, for example, that UN stands for United Nations and UNICEF means the United Nations International Children's Emergency Fund. When using common acronyms, there is no need to explain them. Less familiar usages should be spelled out the first time they are used in a letter and abbreviated thereafter.

A

Advanced Research Projects Agency	ARPA
American Association of Retired Persons	AARP
American Association of University Women	AAUW
American Bankers Association	ABA
American Broadcasting Company	ABC
American Federation of Teachers	AFT
American Federation of Labor and Congress of Industrial Organizations	AFL-CIO
American Institute of Banking	AIB

American Management Association	AMA
American Medical Association	AMA
American Red Cross	ARC
American Society for the Prevention of Cruelty to Animals	ASPCA
American Society of Composers, Authors, and Publishers	ASCAP
American Society of Travel Agents	ASTA
American Standards Association	ASA
American Statistical Association	ASA
Associated Press	AP
Atomic Energy Commission	AEC

B

Board of Education	BE
Board of Tax Appeals	BTA
Bureau of Labor Statistics	BLS

C

Cable News Network	CNN
Central Intelligence Agency	CIA
Civil Aeronautics Administration	CAA
Civil Aeronautics Board	CAB
Civil Service Commission	CSC
Columbia Broadcasting System	CBS
Commissioner of Internal Revenue	CIR
Commodity Stabilization Service	CSS
Comprehensive Employment and Training Act	CETA
Congress of Racial Equality	CORE
Cooperative for American Relief Everywhere	CARE

D

Date of Birth	DOB
Daughters of the American Revolution	DAR
Dead Letter Office	DLO
Department of Public Works	DPW

E

Educational Resources Information Center	ERIC
Equal Rights Amendment	ERA

F

Farm Credit Administration	FCA
Federal Bureau of Investigation	FBI
Federal Communications Commission	FCC
Federal Deposit Insurance Corporation	FDIC
Federal Home Loan Bank Board	FHLBB
Federal Housing Administration	FHA
Federal Mediation and Conciliation Service	FMCS
Federal Power Commission	FPC
Federal Reserve Board	FRB
Federal Reserve System	FRS
Federal Security Agency	FSA
Federal Trade Commission	FTC
Food and Drug Administration	FDA

G

General Accounting Office	GAO
General Services Administration	GSA
Government Printing Office	GPO
Gross National Product	GNP

H

Health, Education, and Welfare Department	HEW
Health Maintenance Organization	HMO
Housing and Home Finance Agency	HHFA
Housing and Urban Development	HUD

M

Master of Business Administration	MBA
Medical Doctor	MD
Military Police	MP

N

National Aeronautics and Space Administration	NASA
National Association for the Advancement of Colored People	NAACP
National Association of Manufacturers	NAM
National Broadcasting Company	NBC
National Bureau of Standards	NBS
National Education Association	NEA
National Labor Relations Board	NLRB
National Mediation Board	NMB
National Office Management Association	NOMA
National Office of Vital Statistics	NOVS
National Organization for Women	NOW
North Atlantic Treaty Organization	NATO
Nuclear Regulatory Commission	NRC

O

Office of Economic Opportunity	OEO
Organization of Petroleum Exporting Countries	OPEC

P

Parent-Teacher Association	PTA
Public Health Service	PHS
Public Housing Administration	PHA

R

Recommended Daily Allowance	RDA
Rural Electrification Administration	REA

S

Securities and Exchange Commission	SEC
Self-addressed Stamped Envelope	SASE
Small Business Administration	SBA
Social Security Administration	SSA
Southeast Asia Treaty Organization	SEATO

Standing Room Only	SRO
Strategic Arms Limitation Talks	SALT

T

Tax Court of the United States	TC
Tennessee Valley Authority	TVA

U

United Nations	UN
United Nations International Children's Emergency Fund	UNICEF
United Nations Educational, Social, and Cultural Organization	UNESCO
United States Information Agency	USIA
United Press International	UPI

V

Veterans Administration	VA

W

World Heath Organization	WHO

Y

Young Men's Christian Association	YMCA
Young Men's Hebrew Association	YMHA
Young Women's Christian Association	YWCA
Young Women's Hebrew Association	YWHA

CHART V: MOST-USED FORMS OF ADDRESS

Company Official

Mr. William Grant, President
P.S. Mencken Corporation
(local address)

Dear Mr. Grant:

Ms. Elizabeth Meade, President
Sears and Ward Company
(local address)

Dear Ms. Meade:

Doctor

Lawrence Langer, M.D.
(local address)

Dear Dr. Langer:

Katherine Karlin, D.D.S.
(local address)

Dear Dr. Karlin:

Lawyer

Mr. David Erikson
Attorney at Law
(local address)

Dear Mr. Erikson:

Ms. Dorothy Evans
Attorney at Law
(local address)

Dear Ms. Evans:

Mayor

Honorable Herbert Vielehr
Mayor of the City of New York
(local address)

Dear Mayor Vielehr:

Honorable Helen Wills
Mayor of the City of Hartford
(local address)

Dear Mayor Wills:

Professor

Professor Frank Oldenberg
(local address)

Dear Professor Oldenberg:

Grace C. Perkins, Ph.D.
(local address)

Dear Dr. Perkins:

Cleric

The Reverend Lawrence Wylie
(local address)

Dear Father Wylie

The Reverend Victoria Benson, D.D.
(local address)

Dear Dr. Benson:

Rabbi Morris Loeb
(local address)

Dear Rabbi Loeb:

CHART VI: COMMON ABBREVIATIONS

ABC	American Broadcasting Company
AFL-CIO	American Federation of Labor and Congress of Industrial Organizations
AMA	American Medical Association
AP	Associated Press
ASCAP	American Society of Composers, Authors, and Publishers
CBS	Columbia Broadcasting System
DAR	Daughters of the American Revolution
ERA	Equal Rights Amendment
FBI	Federal Bureau of Investigation
GNP	Gross National Product
HEW	Health, Education, and Welfare Department
INS	International News Service
NAACP	National Association for the Advancement of Colored People
N.A.M., NAM	National Association of Manufacturers
NBC	National Broadcasting Company
NEA	National Education Association
NOW	National Organization for Women
PSI	Professional Secretaries International
OPEC	Organization of Petroleum Exporting Countries
PTA	Parent-Teacher Association
REA	Rural Electrification Administration
SEC	Securities and Exchange Commission
UNESCO	United Nations Educational, Social, and Cultural Organization
UNICEF	United Nations International Children's Emergency Fund
UPI	United Press International
YMCA	Young Men's Christian Association
YWCA	Young Women's Christian Association
YMHA	Young Men's Hebrew Association
YWHA	Young Women's Hebrew Association

Index

S